VOICES FROM THE 'JUNGLE'

VOICES FROM THE 'JUNGLE'

Stories from the Calais Refugee Camp

Africa,
Ali Haghooi,
Ali Bajdar,
Babak Inaloo,
Eritrea,
Habibi,
Haris Haider,
Majid,
Mani,
Milkesa,
Mohammed Ahmed,
Muhammad,
Omer AKA *Dream,*
Refugees' Voice,
Riaz Ahmad,
Safia,
Shaheen Ahmed Wali,
Shikeb,
Teddy,
Teza,
Zeeshan Imayat
and Zeeshan Javid

Edited by Marie Godin, Katrine Møller Hansen,
Aura Lounasmaa, Corinne Squire and Tahir Zaman

PlutoPress
www.plutobooks.com

First published 2017 by Pluto Press
345 Archway Road, London N6 5AA

www.plutobooks.com

Copyright © Corinne Squire 2017

The right of the individual contributors to be
identified as the authors of this work has been
asserted by them in accordance with the
Copyright, Designs and Patents Act 1988.

British Library Cataloguing in Publication Data
A catalogue record for this book is available
from the British Library

ISBN 978 0 7453 9970 6 Hardback
ISBN 978 0 7453 9968 3 Paperback
ISBN 978 1 7868 0081 7 PDF eBook
ISBN 978 1 7868 0083 1 Kindle eBook
ISBN 978 1 7868 0082 4 EPUB eBook

This book is printed on paper suitable for
recycling and made from fully managed and
sustained forest sources. Logging, pulping
and manufacturing processes are expected to
conform to the environmental standards of the
country of origin.

Typeset by Pluto Press

Simultaneously printed in the United Kingdom
and United States of America

CONTENTS

INTRODUCTION

'Refugees in the Jungle'
by Omer AKA Dream (from Sudan):

Blue,
Like the cloudless sky
On a sun filled day!
Soft,
Like the sleeping child
In a rocking cradle!
Voice,
Like the sounds of grief
Through her gritted teeth!
Coffin,
Like the skeleton carried
In my darkest deepest sleep!
Dream,
Like the birth of my child
With a new mother tongue!
Fear,
Like carrying a heaviness
Over endless trails of fatigue!
Hope,
Like arriving in my home
Where my tears are my own!

The aim of this book is to bring into public view the personal stories of people who lived as refugees during 2015 and 2016 in the Calais camp on the northern French coast, just 26 miles from the UK: a camp that was often called the 'Jungle'.

There have been refugee camps in and around Calais before, and small camps still exist in the area. However, in the spring of 2015, on a landfill site on the outskirts of Calais granted by the local French authorities, a much larger unofficial camp started to grow. This camp, called the 'Jungle' first in French media, but later by its own inhabitants and by the global media, was characterised by very poor housing, little food, and inadequate water, sanitation and health services. There were no police inside the camp; fights often broke out; smugglers operated; blazes ignited by cooking fires, candles and gas canisters frequently destroyed people's shelters and homes. Residents adopted the name 'Jungle' because, many said, humans could not live in such conditions.

As refugees came to Europe in large numbers from the summer of 2015 onward, the 'Jungle' increased in size, defying even a French government demolition that reduced its area by two-thirds in March 2016. The camp was home to 10,000 inhabitants by the time it was closed by the French government in October 2016, and its inhabitants dispersed to housing and processing centres (*Centres d'Accueil et d'Orientation,* CAOS) all over France.

The 'Jungle' was notorious worldwide for its abject conditions. It was a political embarrassment not only for the French government, but also the British, since most residents wanted to come to the UK and had to be stopped by fences, and police and military personnel from boarding trucks, trains and boats. Other residents, including hundreds of unaccompanied minors, had legal claims to come to Britain, which were poorly dealt with. The camp was also an emblem of the impact of forced displacement within Europe, and the mostly ineffectual efforts of European countries to address it.

At the same time, through the efforts of residents and volunteers (rather than statutory agencies), the 'Jungle' developed many formal and informal associations that cooked and served food, built shelters, distributed clothes, provided education, gave basic medical care, and facilitated sports, creative writing, art and music. A street of restaurants and shops constructed and run by the residents themselves also was established. Residents and volunteers often remarked on the strong sense of community and mutual help that they experienced, alongside the camp's lack of basic facilities, its violence and alienation.

For the authors of this book, the 'Jungle' was a home, for a short or a longer time. It was, too, just a moment in their life stories, which started with happy childhoods, or childhoods shaped by war; proceeded through educations obtained after great struggle, often in situations of persecution; and continued through forced flight, either through Iran, Turkey, Greece and the Balkans, or through Sudan and the Sahara Desert to Libya and Italy. After the 'Jungle', the authors, too, moved on. Some are now in the UK; some are claiming asylum in France; a few have gone to other European countries. By October 2016, a handful were still living in the camp, or close by, but those authors also had plans to move elsewhere. The stories the authors have written for this book follow their life paths from their beginnings, into their hopeful futures.

The stories make up a co-authored text. The authors come from Afghanistan, Ethiopia, Eritrea, Iran, Iraq, Pakistan, Sudan and Syria. All lived in the 'Jungle' during 2015–16 – for days, weeks, or in some cases, many months. The authors also edited this book in collaboration with a team from the University of East London (UEL).

The book started from discussions with people who were taking a short accredited undergraduate course on 'Life Stories' offered by UEL in the 'Jungle' in 2015 and 2016, as part of a project called 'University for All'. Writing a book was not the aim of the course, but it quickly became clear that course participants wanted the life stories they were telling and writing to reach a wider audience.

The rationale for the course itself was that education at all levels is a human right guaranteed to refugees, that refugees are severely under-represented in higher education, and that many camp residents were deeply committed to education, and were already studying, or were ready to study, at university level.

The course took place in collaboration with a number of supportive educational associations within the camp: l'École Laïque du Chemin des Dunes, Jungle Books Library, l'École des Arts et Métiers, and the Darfuri School. The UEL team asked these organisations to host the course, used their Facebook pages to announce it, and then travelled around the camp before the course sessions, providing information and leaflets and discussing the classes. Course participants

FIGURE I.I
Directions to L'École Laïque du Chemin des Dunes.
Photo by Haris (from Pakistan).

read life stories by people such as Nelson Mandela, Barack Obama and Malala Yousafzai, as well as poetry, and some broader historical, social and philosophical texts. Many also wrote their own full or partial life stories for the course assignment.

At the same time, the UEL team hosted some photo-workshops with photographers and tutors Gideon Mendel and Crispin Hughes. Called 'Displaces', these workshops allowed camp residents to develop their photographic skills, while at the same time presenting their own view of a camp usually seen only through the selective lens of world media. Residents also wrote and told stories about the pictures they had taken, if they wished. Sometimes, this work became part

FIGURE I.2
Outside Jungle Books Library. Photo by Shikeb (from Afghanistan).

of their Life Stories course assignments,[1] and of this book.

Many participants in the courses and workshops insisted that their life stories needed to be heard by a wider audience. At a time when camp residents and refugees generally were described in popular media as greedy, deceitful and dangerous, they wanted the world to know, instead, the truth about them, and about the obstacles that they had encountered: childhoods in violent places; living as adults amidst war, genocide and persecution; dangerous journeys across mountains, deserts and seas; the arduous, abject conditions

---

1 Webpages describing these projects can be seen on the 'Educating without Borders' website: https://educatingwithoutborders.wordpress.com/. See also https://www.uel.ac.uk/News/2015/12/University-of-East-London-brings-Life-Stories-course-to-Calais-Jungle (accessed 23 October 2016).

of the 'Jungle' – and for many, after Calais, poverty and discrimination in the countries where they claimed asylum.

Yet people also wanted the world to know about the positive aspects of their lives: their close and loving families; their pleasure in and commitment to education; their beautiful countries; their determination to survive in those countries, on their journeys, in the 'Jungle', and in their new home countries; and their commitment to finding safety, working, and helping others. They wanted their stories to move towards a fair, free and non-violent world, and the happiness that this world would bring.

The stories in the book came into being in a variety of ways. Some were simply written and then edited by the authors. A few were translated. Some were written via phone and social media, and worked on further by the authors once they had been put into file documents by the editors. Some accounts were handwritten, typed and printed out by the editors, and later edited by the authors. Some stories were written down by the editors as the authors talked through them, and then checked in their written and later, printed-out form. Sometimes, authors made notes or diagrams, and worked with the editors to build them into full written accounts. In other cases, authors made taped accounts of their lives, which were fully transcribed by the editors, and checked and edited by the authors.

This range of storytelling paths fitted the diverse and often difficult conditions in which authors created their stories. Circumstances ranged from writing on pleasant, warm days, sitting outside the schools of the 'Jungle', or on cold days, beside wood fires set up within the classrooms; some wrote, once they had left Calais, in the more stable and better-quality accommodation of the French CAOS or UK hostels for refugees, while others wrote in sodden, freezing tents or rickety wooden shelters, sunk in the mud of the Calais camp, in the winter of 2015–16.[2]

In talking about the process, many authors described their ideal writing situations, invoking quiet rooms, proper tables, cups of coffee. Even when settled in asylum-seeker accommodation, the uncertainties of the legal process often made writing problematic, since every day was shadowed by uncertainty and waiting: for a call from a lawyer or a letter from the government.

The stories in this book are very close to those originally produced by the authors: editing has been minimal. Authors' own editing removed small parts of stories, changed names for anonymising purposes, clarified points and expanded some sections as time passed. UEL editors have made grammatical changes, some word changes to avoid repetition, and some anonymisations. They included everything that the authors wrote, except in the case of some very long accounts written mainly for Chapter 2. UEL editors also asked for clarification on some points, and invited authors to consider updating and enlarging, or adding sections across the whole book if they wanted to. Within the chapters, editors also added short introductions, and contextualisation of the stories, which have been checked and, where necessary, edited by the authors.

Most of the authors discussed, together with UEL editors, whether to structure the book as a set of personal stories or to set up a series of chapters, moving from the beginnings

---

2 For details of the associations and projects working within the camp, see the Calaid-ipedia website: http://www.calaidipedia.co.uk/

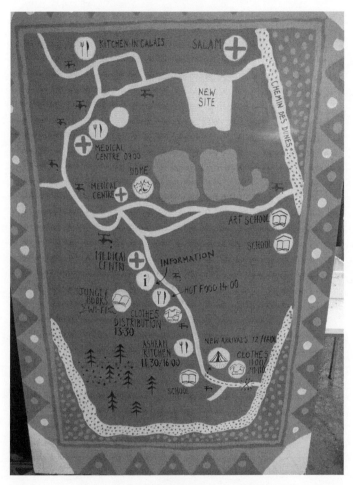

FIGURE I.3
Camp map, early 2016. Photo by Babak (from Iran).

of people's lives and journeys, through the 'Jungle', to their
lives after Calais. The chapter structure used here, following
people's lives from childhood to the present, and towards

the planned and imagined future, was the result of these discussions. The UEL editorial team, along with some authors, discussed how to divide up the stories between the chapters when the divisions were not obvious. This introduction was itself discussed at length with a number of authors, and though it has been written by the UEL editorial team, it contains many points from those discussions.

Authors were free to create stories of any length, to use any forms that they chose – for example, poetry, prose poems, diary entries, photography and drawings, as well as more conventional written accounts – and to concentrate on any topics they wanted. Some chose not to write about home, or their journey, or their time after leaving the camp, or even the camp itself. Some decided not to write about personal issues; some avoided political discussions. For this reason, the book contains some stories that are much shorter than others; some stories with short or no sections in some chapters; some heavily concentrated in one or more chapters; and some dealing with many different topics, even within the same chapter. The authors' own voices are heard in this variability of structure, as well as in what the authors have to say.

In addition, the authors' changing and restricted circum-stances affected the length of their stories, and the topics they wrote about. Some could not or did not want to con-tinue writing when they moved away from the camp, for instance, while some did most of their writing when they left. There were also several authors involved with the book project at the beginning, with whom the UEL editorial team were unable to keep in touch, as well as a small number who were too young to consent to their work's publication, and who did not want to seek consent from those with current responsibility for looking after them. The UEL team hopes to re-establish contact later and to see if those early authors not included here still want to seek a public audience for their work.

Some authors have used their own names for this book project; others have adopted pseudonyms, for a variety of reasons. In some cases, the stories they tell might upset family members or friends, or might put family or friends at risk if they could be connected to the authors. In other cases, the stories contain material that could jeopardise authors' safety, or their asylum claims. The second issue often at stake appears where authors describe spending time in a country which might be viewed as safe, and where they did not claim asylum. Under the Dublin III Treaty agreement and its later updates, refugees must claim asylum in the first safe country they reach. For many authors who have not claimed asylum in France, writing under their own name, about a stay in Calais of any length could have been problematic for this reason.

Almost all the authors in this book are, like most of the people living in the camp, men. The UEL team hosted a visual storytelling workshop with some of the women and children in the camp, but women did not attend the potentially mixed-gender Life Stories classes or the photography workshops, and the team was not able to provide women-only classes or workshops, because of lack of resources and access. We did, however, work with one woman who wanted to provide an account of her situation for this book – but there remains another book, perhaps, for women who were residents of the camp to write. As well, the focus

FIGURE I.4
Inside Jungle Books Library. Photo by Babak (from Iran).

on male camp residents' stories was, we felt, important, in
a situation where male refugees in Calais, and in Europe
generally, were becoming objects of media, political and
popular distrust and fear, depicted as benefits cheats, crimi-
nals and terrorists.

The authors have not written their complete stories; that
would be an impossible goal. These stories are also not
the same stories that the authors would have written for
a different audience – as a family record, for instance, or as
part of a political argument. They are, nevertheless, stories
in which authors strive to be honest. There are differences
in opinion between the authors, between the editors, and
between authors and editors; none of us have tried to edit
out such differences. The stories may therefore 'disagree'

with each other at times. Such conversations are another way in which the 'voices' of the authors are heard in their stories.

In Calais, 'Jungle' residents regularly made strong demands for their voices to be heard, through processes that they could control. Both authors and editors hope that this book meets that demand, in an accessible, but complex and thoughtful way.

Shikeb (from Afghanistan):
This book should tell the story of the bad things that people have endured, but also of how they are seeking justice, freedom and peace.

CHAPTER 1

Home

Mani (from Iran):
Just this sky is with me
From my town, land, country.
Anywhere I am,
this sky is with me.

Dreams and suspended futures

Everyone in the 'Jungle' has left behind a life, loved ones and a home. Some prefer not to write about it, as remembering what they left is too painful. For those who do, memories of childhood and home are coloured by the journey that has led them here, and their everyday existence in the 'Jungle'. Many of the authors wanted to give a detailed and full record of where they came from and why they were forced to leave behind everything that was dear to them. On one hand, these stories help us understand why people from different countries and regions have all arrived in the 'Jungle' at the same time; on the other, they show us what is shared between us all: the dreams we had as children.

Babak (from Iran):
Amongst my childhood memories, I run, with my utmost energy.

Amongst all my colourful days, I stop on the road of faith, and as in? My childhood, I wait for my friends, so we can play.

How sweet was childhood, when all the worry was whether we would find a playmate or not!

When all our trouble was not to go home with dirty clothes!

When all our worry was for the rain not to interfere with our games!

I grew old too quickly. My thoughts grew too wide. It wasn't just me who grew up. It was me as well as others around me who grew old with me. My parents grew older and older. My brother is a man now. My problems also grew bigger. My worries too, and so did my troubles.

I now think instead of playing. Think about how to live. How to be happy.

How to pave the way towards happiness? The more I search for it, the further it goes away. Where is happiness indeed? In my country? In other continents? In another world? I journeyed for miles and I couldn't find it, and I lost it over and over every day.

I realised that happiness is not in a place! Happiness is not what I can find and achieve! Happiness is my thoughts! I have to create it.

I realised life is a canvas and I am the artist. I can be the artist of my own life. I am the one who builds his life, and happiness is the state of soul.

It is likely that I could well be in the best-ever

conditions of life and still feel unhappy, and that I could have the worst conditions and still be happy.

Africa (from Sudan):
When I was a young boy, I had my own dreams, like crazy dreams: I wanted to be like Bruce Lee. When I grew up, as a teenager, I was not following girls and things like that, I just wanted to be at martial arts practice, where I could practice karate or kung fu. I had this special idea of making my own martial art. But I couldn't do this, because already, when I was 20 or 21 I had an operation on my stomach that made me stop doing any self-defence or any sport. After that had become my new way of life, I started to think about how I could make myself a useful person; how I could be responsible; how I could make my life.

Nothing endures but change.

After this operation, I really wanted to graduate from the military academy as an officer, but the operation also stopped this. They will not accept you if you have had any operation on your body. After that I went to university. I would have preferred to read law, but my qualifications did not allow me to enter into the law course. Because of that I chose something near to law, that is, political science.

Eritrea (from Eritrea):
Five years after I was born, Eritrea got its independence. I remember I was eager to go to school – my family also, especially my father. He was excited about me going to school because he was a shepherd, he was not educated, and that is why he wished for me

to be educated. I remember one day where I went to register for primary school in my hometown. The director did not give me the permission to start, because I looked a bit childish, a little too small – especially in height, I was too short. He told me, 'You have to eat one ton.' He said that to express his idea that I should grow bigger. My father got angry because he was eager for me to get registered. I was clever, especially when it comes to reading and calculating in mathematics – subtracting and adding numbers. I was good at that time. My father went to the director and said to him, 'You can ask him anything that you want from the primary school.' The director was surprised: 'What are you saying?' My father said, 'My son is clever, you have to register him. You can compare him with others, you can ask him anything.' The director did what my father told him. He asked me many things, for example, how to read the alphabet, how to add numbers, how to subtract numbers, how to multiply numbers. I answered the correct things and the director registered me immediately. My dad had taught me those things. Although he was a shepherd, looking after animals, he had been learning many things from his uncle. My father's mother had died and his father had gone to discover Ethiopia so my father was living with his grandparents and that is why he was made to be a shepherd of their animals, which he was sad about. He did not want the things that had happened to him to happen for me.

I was the smallest person in that school. I was six years old. I remember I stood out from my class and everyone was congratulating me. From that time onwards, I was encouraged, especially by my father, he was saying, 'You will be a professor', 'You will be a doctor', 'You will be the bright future of this country.' His legacy is strong. He has encouraged me and that was why I became clever. My brothers became clever because they were looking at me.

In 2001, I was a Grade 9 high school student and I was one of the students who went to vocational school. Vocational school in Eritrea is like a college. I stayed for about two weeks but the promises they told us were so different with the ground we faced. Before we joined, they told us that we would be able to participate in the Eritrean Secondary Education Certificate Exam (ESECE) in all subjects after learning for two years. But the director of the vocational school affirmed that there would not be a matriculation exam. It was just a diploma programme. Most of the students we met there were top class ones, and we all decided to return back to our former high schools. After a petition, we did manage to do this, and our former high school director was very happy to accept us.

Then I started a relation with a lady in that school. That lady was the most beautiful student in our high school. Everyone liked her; she was famous for her beauty. Some of the students were gossiping about me: 'How is this boy matched with her?' and some of them were considering me as a lucky person. But some of them were angry and they thought they could make me fail in my educational targets. My relatives told my father about this, and my father had a connection with the teachers and tried to know the truth. But I was increasing my knowledge and my value, and I stood second in all the classes, and everyone was surprised.

One day my father asked me about my relations with the lady and I affirmed that 'We are friends and we like each other.' He was really surprised by my answer and hugged me. In Eritrea, it is not usual to have a friend at that age. We were friends for two years and then we went to the military training centre. Then we didn't see each other for about four months, because in military training, men and women are placed in different camps. After finishing military training, we started our twelfth-grade courses. I met my friend and we hugged each other. Later, I heard a soldier had abused her and took her virginity. I was changed, like a crazy person, and was sad about her. In the military camp, many girls are still facing the same problem. Later I joined the university, but she failed to get in. Then we stopped our friendship; we were simply continuing as a sister and a brother. From that time till I finished my degree, I never had a girlfriend.

Refugees' Voice's story is different from all the other authors'. He came to the UK young and only left this much-desired destination, without adequate travel documents, just as others were arriving from across the sea. As more people live many years in the UK with unresolved status and decide to leave, or are deported, and later try to make their way back, this kind of story is becoming more common. In addition, many other people in Calais had moved there from other European countries such as Hungary and Italy, because their asylum claims there were, like that of Refugees' Voice, not going well. Refugees' Voice's story starts in the UK, when he was a teenager:

Refugees' Voice (from Afghanistan):
When I came to this country, the UK, it was in the year 2000. I came to England when I was 17. That was 16 years ago. I was living in the UK until September 2015 and then I got so fed up and so depressed and so I went to France and then to Italy. I did try to go to university and I even went to college in Bedfordshire. To be honest, back home, I was one of the best students. When I came, I managed to go to college. I started a course which is a fast-track course to get to university. I did it in science but when I was a kid I always wanted to be a doctor, one of the most famous doctors in the entire world. But maybe my luck was not enough for me, maybe I did not work enough. I came to the UK at the age of seventeen and went into year eleven and I might have gone to the best universities in the entire world but at the same time my luck did not work that way. These are some of the things that I had to face.

Teza, by contrast, gave a highly detailed account of his early childhood in his home country, playing games and at home with his family:

Teza (from Iran):
What I remember from when I was very young are some games with my brothers and sisters. My family is big. I have two brothers older than me. One sister and two brothers are younger. I remember playing with a ball, at the park, at home. Sometimes we broke the window. And we also played often in the kitchen all together. They were all my best friends. We didn't

fight. I only went outside sometimes, I liked my home. My mum cooked meat with rice – many people in Iran like this food – and kebabs. These were the best for me. Sometimes she made them at home and sometimes we'd go in the park, and she'd make them there.

I remember the first time I went to school – but only a little. I don't remember if I was scared or excited. I do remember being at school, playing and reading. I read in the class; I was good at reading; I got good marks.

I didn't have best friends at school; my brothers and sisters and my cousins were my best friends. My two cousins lived near; both were neighbours to me. They were going with me, from both sides, to school.

For holidays, we usually went to my grandmother's and grandfather's home – they lived in another city. My father had a very small car, and we all squashed in. My grandmother and grandfather were so pleased when we got there; they gave us presents and nice food. But they died; they are all dead now.

When I was young, I wanted to go in the police. Once a teacher asked and I said, 'Oh, I like the police. I want to be in the police.' I was maybe 6, 7, or 8. When I got older, I wanted to be an engineer, an electrical engineer; I really love electrical stuff, and I like maths.

But last year, something happened, and we had to leave Iran quickly. We didn't even have time to say goodbye. I don't want to write about it.

For many authors, like Teza, there are certain aspects of their past, the lives they left behind and reasons they were forced to leave, that they do not wish to talk about. These memories are too painful at this time, where everything is suspended and the future is unsure. What happened? Why are you here? These are the questions people in Calais 'Jungle' are forced to answer over and over again at each border crossing, to each police officer and state official, and to curious journalists. What is the right answer, the answer each one of these interrogators wishes to hear about the past, and why they came?

Mothers

Mothers, for many young men who arrived in Calais, are the real heroes of their childhood. Mothers have also often been the ones to push their children to leave, to look for a better life and safety. Sons feel they have let down their mothers, as they weren't able to protect them. They lied to their mothers about being in the 'Jungle', as they didn't want their mothers to worry. Young men miss their mothers, feel guilty for abandoning them and, at times, even blame their mothers for sending them away.

Habibi (from Afghanistan):
My mother called me, and I told her that my father was fine and that I would be coming home. I was hiding what had happened because my mother has high blood pressure and diabetes; she was sick too, and there were my younger brothers to think of as well. So I handled the situation. I thought to myself, 'It's okay, you can deal with this because you are a senior: If you will cry, your brothers will cry.' I was

thinking on and on of how I would tell my mum about my father's death. I took the body of my father home to Pakistan. I knocked the door at our house and my mother opened the door. She asked me where my father was. I said to her, that he was fine but still at the hospital. 'Tomorrow they will discharge him and I will bring him home', I said to her. She saw the tears in my eyes and asked, 'What happened?'

Shikeb (from Afghanistan):
I went to my mum's house; the time was two o'clock in the night; I kicked the door. My mum was saying, 'Who is that?' I said, 'Mama, it's Shikeb.' She cried, 'What's happened?' I said, 'I've come, mum, I so miss you.' And she told me, 'Okay my son, you must not come here. You must go to another country.' 'Mum, I will not go, because I am happy with you.' My big brother was addicted to heroin. My sister was married. My mum was alone. 'I am not going away', I said. My mother told me, 'You go!'

Everything was okay; I had everything in Afghanistan. But I said to my mum, 'Okay mum, I will go to another country, I am not coming back to Afghanistan, never. I will make my life somewhere else.' Sometimes my mum calls me: 'Shikeb, how are you?' 'Mum, okay! I have everything, even a car; I am going to university.' But I am living in the 'Jungle'.

Ali Bajdar (from Iraq):
When I think about the past and my mother, I feel like crying. I miss her a lot. I want to come to England, I want to study and have a life there, but if

I find out where my mother is, I will go back to be with her. That is the most important thing for me. I miss her so much. She is old and cannot work so she needs my help. I hope she is safe somewhere. Maybe she is in a camp. If I knew where she was, I would go back. I am also sick and cannot work but we would figure something out. We used to take care of each other. It wouldn't matter. I don't want her to live alone. My father and my brother are also back there, but they have each other. My sister is married, she has her family. My mother has no one.

Ali Bajdar's father and brother were working in a bigger city some distance away from their home village at the time, as opportunities in the village were limited. Due to ill health, Ali Bajdar was not able to work, and so he stayed behind to look after his mother.

Safia, the only woman who took part in the book project, had arrived in Calais with her husband and children; she gave an account of separation from her whole family, and of her husband's lack of contact with his family, too:

Safia (from Afghanistan):
I don't communicate with my family back home because my dad is dead and my mum, she lives in a rural province and we can't reach it on mobile and so I don't know if she is good. My husband does not call as well because it is too expensive.

Babak (from Iran):
People go to the highest point in the camp to call home and talk to their families. In the containers, the

FIGURE I.I
*People go to the highest point in the camp to call home
and talk to their families. Photo by Babak (from Iran).*

signal is not good. We don't have the internet here,
only sometimes in the 'Jungle'. They go the highest
point to have a good signal. I also go there to call my
mum. When I am talking with her and explain I am
in a container she says, 'Why a container? Is it small?'
I say 'No'; I try to go somewhere else to have a good
wi-fi quality, and then I explain good things to her. I
tell her that I am good. I don't want to show my family
what is happening here. I always tell that I am good
and that I am living in a house. My mother doesn't
have Facebook, so most things my family don't know.

Daesh, the Taliban and Al-Qaeda

Some of the regions from which people come to the 'Jungle' have been affected by the rise of Islamist fundamentalist groups for decades; in other regions, the phenomenon is more recent. For those fleeing these groups, it makes little difference whether they be ISIS, Al-Qaeda, or Taliban – some cannot even say for sure who it was that murdered their families, threatened their lives, or are forcibly recruiting young men from their villages. An important question they ask us Europeans is, what should we do? If we stay in our countries, the authors say, one of these groups will make us join them. If we refuse, they will kill us, or kill our families. If we join them, Europeans and Americans will bomb us. We come here, and we are told to go back home. Where should we go?

> *Zeeshan Imayat (from Pakistan):*
> We have a lot of problems, but Europeans say that Pakistan has no more problems, they say that Islamabad is safe, so all European countries, they don't give papers for Pakistani refugees. But the Pakistani government does not follow what the Europeans say. We are near to Afghanistan. We are a minority in Pakistan, we are only 20 per cent. I couldn't stay in Islamabad because we are Pathans. I am a target in Pakistan.

> *Zeeshan Javid (from Pakistan):*
> We didn't go and fight, we didn't protect our home. We didn't know how to kill another human being. My

dad told me to leave. He said, 'Otherwise Taliban will take you and they will wash your brain.'[1]

Ali Bajdar (from Iraq):
My father and brother worked in a big city far from the village. They were the providers for the family and had to go there to earn money for our food. At times during the war, they couldn't come back to the village. We saw them maybe once a month. We heard about the war on the radio, heard about how Daesh kills people, how old people and young women are being captured and killed. You can even see it on Facebook. When you hear and see these things, when you know what they are capable of, you also know what you need to do when Daesh arrives – you need to run. One morning at 7am, we heard shooting in the village and people were yelling, 'Daesh is coming!' I ran back home to look for my mother. My mother was not in the house, I could not find her. The only thing we could do was to run, so we did and I had to leave without her. We couldn't bring anything with us, there was no time.

---

[1] Zeeshan Imayat and Zeeshan Javid are cousins from the same region of Pakistan. They are Pathans, a Pashto-speaking minority living in the North West Frontier Province at the Afghanistan-Pakistan border. According to Minority Rights Group International, the Pathan population has been adversely affected by the war on terror and American military intervention in the area. Military activity in the region has led many people to become more fundamentalist in views and increased the local support for Taliban. A pro-Taliban religious coalition, el-Muttahida Majlis-e-Amal, has been in power in this autonomous area since 2002. They have introduced strict religious laws and the area has seen an increase in repression of women's and minority rights, and an alarming amount of religious and sectarian violence. For more information see http://minorityrights.org/minorities/pathans/ (accessed 28 July 2016).

Shikeb (from Afghanistan):

I was three years old; my father was killed by somebody. I think they were Taliban. My father had been
to Russia, and had come back to Afghanistan. He was
doing something commercial; he was a businessman. I
don't know much about this. My mother just told me,
'Your father was killed by someone from the Taliban.'

I was working there for two years in Afghanistan as
a nurse. And then someone from the USA told me, in
the office, 'You come in the jail and work as a section
nurse. I will give you more money.' So I went into the
jail. Nine months I worked in the jail. Then I went to
the village. But my relatives were Taliban.

First, let me explain: Our doctors were not working
in the jail, because the jail is such a dangerous place in
Afghanistan. All the prisoners are Taliban and Daesh.
I worked in this place, but I did not tell my mum,
'Mum, this place is dangerous.' My mum was happy.
The USA gave me more money, and everything was
good. I was head of clinic in the jail, because the doctors were not there – it was too dangerous for them. I
was working – okay, no problem. But a relative called
me, saying 'You are working with pagan people, I
will kill you, Shikeb.' I was smiling, asking, 'Why?' I
thought they were joking. I was helping people.

I went to the village; they all attacked me. Somebody
went to my mother and said, 'Your son is against the
Taliban; they want to kill him.' My mother cried to
everybody not to kill her son. Some people came from
the Taliban, and they arrested me. My mother cried
and cried, 'Shikeb will not continue working in this
job, I promise everyone.'

Then I went back to my job. For one year I didn't go to my village to see my mum. But one day I thought, 'Okay, today I want to go to be with my mum; I miss my mum.' So I went. On the way there, two motorcycles came up behind me with people with guns, everything, and they did something to my mouth, held something against it – I don't know exactly what happened. At twelve midnight, hours later, I woke up, in a big room. I broke the glass in the room, in the window, to get out. You can still see the scars on my hand.

I don't know what it is to have a father. I never saw my father. I don't know what I am doing in the 'Jungle'. No family, no brothers, nothing. Twenty years old; and I lost my big brother to heroin. I love the people in the 'Jungle'; but those people before said, 'For me, you are pagan.' Okay, I am 'pagan', you are Muslim.

Safia (from Afghanistan):
My life in Afghanistan was good because I was a nurse and my husband is a doctor. He was working with NGOs in Jalalabad. I was working in hospitals and my life was very good because I had everything. I had everything, but then we got some problems. Our life was good but it is just with the Taliban. They are killing people. They have some problems with the people who do have an education, like doctors and engineers. If you work with NGOs or with the army, the Taliban do target these people. They are punishing all the people who are working with them because they [the NGO people] are not Muslims. And then because of that, the Taliban would think that you are

not a good Muslim. But we are Muslim; but if you are working with an NGO, then they would think you are not Muslim, especially if you are working with an American NGO. So because of that, it became quite scary. And we decided to leave Afghanistan. One of my brother-in-laws is in America, another one is in Austria, another one in Italy. We are here in Calais. My husband's cousin is in England. Everyone is just gone. My brother-in-law was also working for NGOs in Afghanistan.

Our country is our country. It is my culture but because I had some problems I left my country. If I did not have any problems, then I would have stayed in my country. It is my country, a very beautiful country. But I don't want to go back. My country could be good without the Taliban. There is danger all the time during the day and during the night. And for educated women, it is really hard. With uneducated women or with stay-at-home women, this is all right, no problem.

Shaheen (from Afghanistan):
I am writing because we are suffering from wars for 35 years. I was born in the war, I grew up in the war, and there is still war in my country; and now my children are suffering from war.

I am from a province near the Pakistani border.[2] I opened my eyes in a poor family. It was very difficult to get education, but my father was dreaming for me that I would get an education. I was the first child. So my

---

2 The names of the exact geographical locations have been removed from this account to protect the personal details of the author.

father struggled so much for me to get an education. At last, he admitted me in a school, and I finished my secondary school with so many difficulties. After that, I did medicine for two years only. Because of my economic problems, I then left my education.

However, I used to work as a teacher. I taught English, for free, to the boys in my village, as a volunteer worker. I was running a general store, with a few types of medicine for first aid. Because our village is far from the main city, there is no hospital or clinic. So I was checking blood pressure, giving injections, and putting in drops for people, for free.

I started work with a company. The company was supplying fuel to the American bases. I sold some of my property to buy a fuel tanker and for fuel supply, and I started working with the company to support my family – I have five children.

I worked with them for two years. I was taking fuel from the main city in my province to another province up north, approximately 150km away. On the way there were two police check posts.

One evening, my boss called me, and told me, 'Tomorrow we will supply fuel to a province in the east.' I said, 'Okay.' So I told my father, 'Tomorrow I am going east; let my younger brother come with me.' He said, 'Okay, it will be Friday; he is not going to school, so he can go with you.'

That night, somebody knocked at our door. My father went to answer. After a while he called, 'Come here, someone wants to talk with you.' At the door, I saw one of the people from my village. He said, 'You're going tomorrow?' I said, 'Yes, I am going east.' He said,

'I will go with you because I want to visit my friends there.' I said, 'Okay, I am leaving at 4 o'clock in the morning'. He said, 'Okay.'

We started moving, at 4 o'clock, eastward. My brother worked with me as a conductor on the tanker. After about two hours' drive, we reached a large town. My village neighbour told me, 'Stop here for a while; I am going to bring one of my friends from here.' I said, 'I am going to be late, please do it fast!' He said, 'Okay, in just two minutes I will be back.' After a while, he returned with one of his friends. I saw the man was covered with a big blanket of the kind Afghani people use in winter. Under the blanket he had a Russian gun, a Kalashnikov. He sat with us, and after some minutes of driving he ordered, 'Turn to the right.' I said, 'I can't drop you because I am late.' He said again, 'Turn to the right!' I stopped the tanker, he put the gun to my head and said, 'You have to turn.' So I turned into a street, where after just five minutes there was a big villa. Two persons opened the gates and I drove inside.

There were about twelve persons with heavy weapons there. The man in the blanket told us to stop and get down from the tanker, so I got out. Two more persons then came and told me, 'Our commander wants to talk with you.' So they took me to the commander. He said, 'You have to do a job for us.' I asked, 'What kind of work?' He said, 'I am giving you a box, just take it to my men waiting on the road for you.' I said, 'What's in the box?' He replied, 'Weapons and explosive things.' I said, 'I can't do it.' From behind, suddenly one of his men hit me very powerfully. I shouted and cried, 'I have small children and a family; I can't do it.' He said,

'Okay, if you don't do it, I will shoot your brother.' I kept quiet for a while. When I saw the eyes of my brother, they were full of tears; he was just like one of my children. I said, 'Okay, I will do it.' He responded, 'If you make any problems for us, I will shoot your brother on the spot.' I said, 'No, no, I will not make problems for you.' Then they put the box in my tanker. That was the last time I looked towards my brother's eyes; he was just looking at me.

After some minutes of driving, I was thinking, 'What should I do?' At last I thought, 'I can't kill a lot of people.' So I decided to tell the police at the checkpoint. When the police came near to me, they knew me, and they said, 'Hello, hi' to me. One of them said, 'You're looking very sad.' I agreed, 'Yes, I am very sad', and I told them the whole story. They checked the box; it was full of weapons and explosive things. Then they told their commander, and took four police rangers to go towards the villa where the Taliban were. I was with them. When we were near to the villa, the Taliban started firing on us. So the fighting began between them. After twenty minutes, the police took over the villa. When we went inside, I saw my brother lying on the ground. As I came near to him, I realised he was dead. They had shot him in the head. I cried and shouted, 'What has happened with my brother!' That was a very panicky and hard time for me, the worst in my life. I called my father and told him, 'Come and take my brother's body.' Then the police took me back to the police station, and after some hours they released me and I went home. My mother was crying and shouting so much; she was saying to me, 'Why did you take my son with you?' She hugged me and cried and cried the whole night. Our whole family was very sad about my brother.

The villager I knew and the Taliban commander called me and said, 'We killed your brother; you made a problem for us, and we will do the same to you.' I was very scared. I told my father. He said, 'My son, you have to leave the country soon, I don't want to lose you.' After the funeral of my brother, we left our home for another district. But on the second night, at 2 o'clock, a friend called to say, 'Some people burned your house.' So I recounted this to my parents, who told me, 'Now you must leave the country.' Then I started my journey towards Europe.

I left my wife, my five kids, and my parents. Again we sold some of our property – all of our property – and I deposited $10,000 with the agent. So I started my journey.

Waiting for asylum

Refugees' Voice too came to the UK originally to escape conflict in Afghanistan, but he was impelled to leave the UK, the country many authors were trying to reach, because he was depressed about his long wait for a resolution to his case – one that had also not been well handled. This author's account speaks for increasing numbers of other refugees within Europe who are driven to move because they are stranded, often for decades, with no resolution of their asylum claims:

Refugees' Voice (from Afghanistan):
Through friends and friends' connections, many people advised me to go to Europe and apply for asylum in Europe. In fact, many things went wrong with me. When I came, I was 17 but one friend advised me to say that I was 18. So I think if I had told them that I was 17 at that time, back in 2000, it would have been better for me. All the Afghans who came to the UK between 1999 and 2001 managed to get exceptional leave to remain, but I made a mistake. I have always been a people's person. When I first came, the Home Office sent me to Bedfordshire. At the time, I was the first Afghan living in that town so at that time I was helping people out as I was already speaking English, filling in people's forms. When you are helping everybody else, you start forgetting about yourself. And I think that's what happened with me. To be honest I have written so many letters for people; my spoken English is good too. I have written so many letters on behalf of people and based on these letters, people have been granted leave to remain. I remember one guy back in 2004. I wrote letters for him and he got leave to remain and then a few years after he went back to Afghanistan, he got married and then he got British citizenship. But I was still at the same square, standing. So anyhow, that's why I decided to go to Europe where people told me that I could get the documents very easily, and that's why I went to Italy.

Democracy

What is democracy and who is it for? All of the authors come from countries where democracy is just a dream for some, and an unknown European concept for others. These stories, mostly from Africa, talk about political repression, detention and corruption. In the absence of democracy, the authors have struggled for rights and freedoms for themselves, their families and their neighbours. State repression has not silenced them; on the contrary, repression, detention and torture has made them more acutely aware of the need for democracy and political freedom.

Eritrea (from Eritrea):
I said my name is Eritrea, and I am representing the passing of many challenges along the way, under suppression and in prison. I will start from my childhood. I was born in 1986 in the southern part of Eritrea. At that time, Eritrea was a colony of Ethiopia and many families were under bad conditions. It was a bad situation at that time. Many people died. People were murdered. At that time, the government of Ethiopia was not democratic. It was a dictatorship like our government now and that is why many people struggled.

When I was about four-and-a-half years old, I will never forget that at that time, I was always going with my father to cultivate our farm lands. One day my father was ploughing and a lot of Ethiopian soldiers were passing through that way. I always remember one of the Ethiopian troops came to my father and spoke with him, and immediately clutched him by the neck.

And another one came and targeted his gun at my father's face. I shouted loudly but no one was coming to help us. The troops beat and stoned my father and he fell down. His backbone was harmed. I remember one soldier came and ordered them to let my father go. At that moment, I didn't have any option. The only thing that I did was hugging my father and crying a lot. Because of that, my father suffered a lot of pain, until eventually he was cured. This was the worst event that I saw in my childhood.

Ultimately, in the middle of 1991, the Eritrean People's Liberation Front defeated the Ethiopian regime. I remember many of our mothers were happy and celebrated, but some of them were unable to believe the event and said, 'Are those who are coming with military trucks and tanks really our children?' Anyway it was a great day.

But now, the Eritrean regime is betraying our heroes and our martyrs. Because as is seen on TV and shown in the media, many Eritreans are escaping from their homeland and following a desperate path, due to the dictator's rule.

Moreover, in 2000, there was a war between Eritrea and Ethiopia. It is known as the 'third aggression' of Ethiopian forces over Eritrea, but this name is given only by the Eritrean government and the people. At that time, a lot of bombs were launched by the Ethiopian forces into Eritrea, especially at the border with Ethiopia. Villages were attacked by helicopters and missiles and our village was one of them.

Most of the people fled to the central part of Eritrea called Debarwa. My mother was pregnant and my father found a house to rent. There, we faced many problems. I remember one day I went outside and watched a Euro 2000 football match. It was night when I returned to the house we rented, but the owner of the house locked the compound. I was knocking on the door, and the woman who owned it shouted at me and told me to go away from there. My mother was stressed, and begged her to let me in. At that moment there was an English proverb that I knew, and that silently I said: 'At the time of prosperity friends are plenty; at the time of adversity no one helps among twenty.'

These were the difficulties that I faced in my teenage years. As I explained before, by the time of my high school graduation, I had faced many problems due to the Eritrean regime.

I am Christian, and one day I was reading the Bible in my home and other people were coming to debate the Bible. We were talking about the apostles. I do not know if someone saw us but the police came and took us to a prison. We were there for five months and after that, they took us to a garden to work there. I had an opportunity to escape, together with one of my friends and we told each other that it would be better if we died rather than to be in prison there. We were running and we could hear the soldiers shooting.

Our government is very cruel, they do not care about the people, there is no press and there are no rights. It is slavery. It reminds me of the slavery in the eighteenth century; it is like that, it is a pity. We cannot resist. The only option is to leave the country. Our parents, our dads and our mums, have spent their lives to bring us independence and they do not want any further civil war among the people. That is why there is no struggle inside the country; they are afraid of civil war. They prefer to leave their country. I think it is not the best option. Leaving the country means you are encouraging the dictatorship and their rules, but for those who start to fight against the government, they will take them immediately and imprison them. The situation is demoralising the people.

In Eritrea, Pentecostalism is not allowed. If you are a member of the Pentecostal Church, immediately the government will imprison you. The Pentecostal people are considered the knives of the American government. It is not good. I was imprisoned for about five months because they accused me of being Pentecostal. They are racists. They do not know about any humanity, the government.

The worst thing that is happening in Eritrea is the open bribery. Culturally, in our society, it is considered an evil thing. We are lagging behind instead of uprising. Our parents, they keep their mouths shut, they have pain inside, but they do not have any other option. They say that the government has betrayed the mothers, betrayed the heroes, who have sacrificed themselves in the struggle against the Eritrean government.

Milkesa (from Ethiopia):
The Oromo are indigenous to Ethiopia, northern Kenya, and parts of Somalia. The Oromo make up the largest portion of the Ethiopian population. Oromos have their own unique language, culture, history and civilisation.

The language is called 'Afaan Oromo' which means 'Oromo language'. The Oromo language belongs to the Afro-Asiatic family. It is the largest language in Africa next to Arabic, Hausa and Swahili. The Oromo use the Latin alphabet. It has vowels and consonants like English language. For example, the vowels are A, E, I, O and U, while the rest are consonants. It has upper and lower cases.

The Oromo people governed themselves using a unique African democratic system, called the 'Gada'. Gada system is an indigenous democratic socio-political system of the Oromo.

My father was of Ethiopian Oromo[3] ethnicity. Both of my parents were born and raised in the eastern part of Ethiopia.

My father was a farmer. He used to produce cereal crops and coffee in Dadar district, which is in the eastern part of Ethiopia. My parents used to generate their income from these assets. My mother was a housewife.

My father was an active member of the Oromo Liberation Front (OLF) when OLF was part of the 1991 to 1992 Transitional Government of Ethiopia. Based on the charter proclaimed in 1991, my father used to support the OLF financially, in order to build infrastructure such as dispensaries, schools and roads during the Transitional period. My father also used to attend Oromo meetings in his birth district in Ethiopia.

Following the OLF's withdrawal from the then

3 Ethnic group mostly living in the Oromia state in Ethiopia. There are an estimated 38m Oromo living between Ethiopia, Kenya and Somalia and they account for 40 per cent of the population of Ethiopia.

Transitional Government in mid-1992, the Tigray[4] People's Liberation Front (TPLF) government's intelligence services arbitrarily arrested and detained my father from 1993–95, and then, in 1996 and in 1997, in prison. On the alleged grounds of his continued support for the OLF, he was finally killed in 2000. All our properties were confiscated by the current Ethiopian government on the grounds of my father's OLF involvement. My family was denied the right to take my father's corpse and to bury him. My mother was also killed in 2000.

From my early years of age, there was always a volatile interest from the security forces in my parents and me because of our suspected OLF involvement. The soldiers would come to our house and threaten my parents at night. I would worry after twilight, as the dusk fell.

I have two brothers and a sister. The other things about my childhood, my life with my mum and dad, school – these personal things are terrible stories.

There was a General Election in Ethiopia in May 2005. This time coincided with the time I completed high school.[5] According to the local government authority's plan at that time, I had to get a recommendation letter from the government administrative office in order to go to university or college. This was a time when one of the Ethiopian government's parties, called the Oromo People's Democratic Organization (OPDO), needed to train students to campaign in the countryside to spread government policies in order to

4 Ethnic group of the ruling party in Ethiopia
5 The name of the town has been removed to protect personal details of the author.

obtain votes and win the election. I was among those trained students to be sent to villages to campaign for OPDO. I accepted and campaigned, just because I wouldn't have been issued with the recommendation letter to go into higher education if I had refused.

But most of the people I canvassed voted for the opposition party, called the Oromo People's Congress (OPC), which was against the Ethiopian government.

Attacks on the OPC political opposition party members and other dissenters persisted through 2005, with mass arrests of ethnic Oromo civilians, including me. I was arbitrarily arrested in June 2005 on charges of involvement with the OLF. I was accused of inspiring the people to vote for the OPC in order to achieve indirect OLF rule, without any indication of a reason for the accusation. I was interrogated about the alleged relation I had with the OLF against my government. I was at risk of torture and ill treatment. In May 2006 I was released, with stern warnings.

I was elected to the committee of the Oromo students' union when I became a second-year student at the Teachers' Training Centre in September 2008. The students' union's objectives were first, around social life, to entertain our college students' cultural diversity, motivation and differentiations, with mutual respect, through our union; and second, to develop Oromo culture.

While I was working on the committee, conflict broke out between Tigrayan students and Oromo students, which resulted in an open fight between the two groups at the centre of the college. The reason at that time was because one of the Tigrayan students presented a text in the class with derogatory words called 'Galla', the defamatory name used against those of Oromo ethnicity. I was arrested by armed military force at daybreak and was detained at the military barrack for eight months without any charge, credible evidence, or court decision. During my incarceration, my torturers speculated that our students' union had successfully created a clandestine collaboration with the OLF against my government. I was also accused of mobilising students against conflict. I was severely tortured and persecuted during my stay in the prison. I received physical and mental torture. My torturers took me to the river. They tied a rope around my neck and held me under the water. They pulled me out and then beat me with a wooden stick and rifle butts and muzzles. My lower ribs were fractured among other injuries. But I was free and innocent of the Ethiopian authorities' bizarre accusation of mobilising students to be initiated into the OLF, which I knew nothing about. I was released after I was forced to sign a document to forfeit my life if any suspicion of me having my relation with the OLF would develop.

After my release this time, the security forces were following my footsteps.

After I graduated from college in June 2010, I was employed as an Oromo language teacher at a school in the area where I was born. During my work as a teacher in this school, I became coordinator of the Oromo Language and Cultural Club. As a club, we – other teachers and I – arranged different cultural concerts which I think adversely affected what government officials thought of me. There were government spies who were learning in different grade levels in the school. They reported every word I spoke to the government office. The local authority officer in the town used to question me about all the topics I taught in the school, to the extent that I suspected my own shadow. These spies watched all teachers' activities and reported to the government office.

Based on the Oromo language subject, I taught my students about their Oromo cultural heritage, and I and other Oromo teachers organised different cultural shows.

I arranged different cultural shows in order for everyone to learn about the cultural and social identity of my Oromo people. I felt that I was responsible for developing and protecting my culture, as I was coordinator of the Cultural Club, and an Oromo language teacher. However, the Ethiopian government doesn't want the development of Oromo culture and language.[6]

I continued intensively teaching Oromo language and hosting the concerts, because it is declared in the Ethiopian Constitution that everyone has the right to develop their language and culture. But the Ethiopian government doesn't want the Oromo language and culture to be developed, unlike those of some other Ethiopian ethnicities. Just because I am from the Oromo ethnicity, government authorities linked my cultural activities with the OLF, simply in order to restrict me from developing it, because of their racial

6 The Ethiopian government's suppression of Oromo culture is well documented in an Amnesty International report of 2014. The full report is available to download from https://www.amnesty.org/En/documents/Afr25/006/2014/En/ (accessed 3 August 2016).

prejudice. But I continued, because I was responsible for developing my cultural identity, which doesn't have any negative effect on my government's political life.

As part of this severe social and cultural suppression by the Ethiopian authorities, I was accused of inciting Oromo students in the school to support the OLF against my government – an accusation which is itself commonly used as a motive to justify my ethnicity's social and cultural suppression. Nothing I taught my students was outside the Ethiopian educational curriculum. But the Ethiopian authorities continued to severely restrict the basic civil right to develop Oromo culture and language. Government authorities forced me to drop Oromo culture and to teach Tigrayan culture – the culture of the ethnicity to which the ruling party belongs. But I refused their dead plan, and continued teaching Oromo culture.

Four intelligence officers came to the school in March 2011 by car. They all wore police uniform. They arrested me at my school and detained me in prison, just for my teaching of Oromo culture. I was accused of working as an OLF activist against my government. I was severely tortured during my stay in the prison. I was put in a cramped, confined and dark cell. Later I was taken to the interrogation room for investigation. I was hanged upside down. I received intermittent assault and physical violence. I received foot and buttock whipping. Prison guards tied heavy weight to my testicles and forced me to kneel down and then to move on my knees. Sometimes my torturers would put a sack over my head, tie it around my throat with rope, submerge me in the river, and then beat me. They pricked me with a sharp needle on my feet, on the tips of my fingers and on my genitals. They sprayed diluted chilli into my genitals and my eyes. When I innocently tried to convince them by requesting them to produce any piece of tangible evidence that shows my association with the OLF, my torturers said to me, 'You are a great threat to our government as you are from the Oromo ethnicity.' So I learned that my being created as a person of Oromo ethnicity is a big crime in Ethiopia; I am an unnecessary animal to that country.

Africa (from Sudan):
The government wanted me to work for them, they chose the people who have connections with the students to ensure them their presence there, on the campus. I refused, like four or five times, to be with them, because I knew they were lying. They said things to me about 'democracy' or something like that. Even after I graduated, really, I took like three or four years to get my certificate from the university because the university had already seen the blacklist – you could see that my name was on the blacklist. After I had paid a lot of money, I was able to get my certificate.

When I started to think about helping people, it was really at university. While I was still at university I started a little charity union; we were called the political science union. We were twenty people. It was my idea; I wouldn't like to say I was the boss – I was the organiser. I knew among the students exactly who needed money to pay for university; I knew who was coming from the villages and hadn't found a place to stay. I went around to many charity places to ask, to collect money for these people, to help them. That was what made the government come and say, 'You will come with us!' When I refused, that became a big problem. Like two or four times I said, 'No, no, no!' That made them destroy this charity union, my little union.

After graduation, we should take military training. We have military service; you go to a military camp. The military service is not just training. You are part of the army, there is no difference between you and a real soldier. Unless you do that, you cannot work. Unless you do your military service, you can't move on, you can't get your university certificate. If you remember, I said I was suffering for three years before I could get my certificate. I should serve for one year – after that I should get the certificate. When I was near to serving one year, they said, I don't know, that something had happened that made me need to resume military service again, from the beginning. They said, 'No, no, go to the centre', and they sent me back. This was because of my union work.

After that, when I went to the Ministry of Work to ask for a job, they refused it. I could never work for the government in any way. Okay, that made me drop my certificate outside of my life – it was useless for me. I never tried to use it again to get work. I was 25 or 26.

Work in the civil service would have been the best option for me; the private sector didn't take on anyone graduating in political science.

When I started my own business, I moved to another place three or four hours away, because I had already discovered that some people were following me, even sometimes when I went out from the university. My father said it would be safer to move from there to another place. My entire family had to move with me. I have one real brother and five half-brothers. It's not like here – when you are 18 or 20 you choose your life and you stay alone. In Sudan you can't stay alone until you are married, and even then you live close to your family.

After eight months you should be able to get your services, like electricity, water and so on. We had already paid, but after three more months, no services had come to us. I knew all my neighbours around me, so I organised a little meeting, again. I can't say no. We had a little meeting in a mosque, I took notes and went to the local government, and asked them, 'Why is this happening?' After two days exactly, someone from the government came in my store. It was in March, they asked me, 'Where is your tax receipt?' which I showed them. 'Okay, you must pay your taxes.' 'For what?' They said, 'For next year.' I had already paid my taxes three or four weeks ago. How can it be that I should pay for next year? I might live, or not live, in that time. 'You will pay!' they said. 'No, I will never pay', I said. We were shouting in each other's faces. I told him, 'If you want money, you can come and take it by force. Not like this, I will never pay. Or I will close this store; I don't need it.' He said, 'You will pay, ah, you will see.' 'Okay, show me', I said.

After these things, after one day, someone was knocking on my door. I went to it to receive maybe a friend, something like that. When I opened my door I saw someone who then covered my face. After that,

48

four or five persons put me in a pickup. They drove me in a particular direction for maybe 15 minutes. After that they came for me and I went into a room, three by four metres. You can't see anything in this room. You could just hear some screaming. For maybe two days, I didn't know why I was there and where I was exactly. I had no idea whether it was really night or when it was morning. I was not able to tell exactly the time. If someone sat and lit a light, you could only see them by that light.

They started asking about my support of another (opposition) political party. They said to me that I was collecting money for these people for them to let them buy weapons. 'I didn't do this.' 'You had like a charity or something like that.' 'I didn't do it.' 'You did.' 'I didn't do it.' 'You did. You did.' After a while, what they say becomes real. They took their revenge over me. By force. They did many things that were not good. After two weeks exactly, my uncle talked to an officer and asked him how to get me out. He should pay to get me out. When he had already paid, he came to me, and told me, 'You are here, ok. Tomorrow you will meet a judge. Just say yes and sign the documents they give you. That is all you should do.' I was prepared to do anything to get out. If he had asked me to kill, I would have done it, to get out. Okay, I just saw one person at the table and I said yes. I signed. When I got out, I asked him what things exactly I had said yes to. 'Okay, you signed and you said yes, that you were supporting the opposition party. You also said yes, that you will come here every week to sign in. And yes, that you are not allowed to go out of this country and also that you cannot visit any doctor, never. And you cannot tell anyone about these things.' I said, 'Okay. Yes. Yes, yes.'

When I was there, he also said four words: 'If you can survive.' 'What do you mean?' I asked. He said, 'I am not going to guarantee these people.'

Majid (from Iran):
I am interested in describing the bad situation in my country. I am so angry about it. Especially for young people, it's very difficult.

In general, I can say that there are no freedoms in Iran. Many guys who are here in Calais are escaping from wars, civil wars and miseries which they face in their countries. But for Iranians, it is totally different. The problem of Iran is the lack of freedom – any sort of freedom: freedom of speech, freedom for your personal life, freedom of religion.

There are lots of restrictions and limitations in Iran. As examples, you can't have a boyfriend or a girlfriend. Drinking alcohol is prohibited. We haven't any night-club, even one, in Iran. Going to parties is forbidden. If the agents of the secret police catch you, they put you in jail.

Another example: you can't access satellite channels freely. If they find you have a satellite dish on the roof of your house, they destroy that. So you always have to hide your satellite dish.

Another example: you can't listen to music in your car, at any volume. But your car is your own personal environment. If you increase the volume, they stop you and say it is against the rules of Islam.

The problem is that they say many things are against the rules of Islam. They interpret everything according to their opinions.

Another important thing, especially for women: They have to wear the hijab. It's compulsory. Most Iranian women don't like it. Young women resist these rules; they want to live freely. It's an Islamic rule to cover your hair, but it should be optional. It's not good; everything that is forced, does not have a good result.

It's all interpretation. If you go to different Islamic countries, their versions of Islam are totally different. For instance, in Turkey, which is over 90 per cent Muslim, many women do not cover their hair.

I have lived more than three decades in Iran. When I look back, I think that things are improving every year. They have reduced their restrictions every year. Maybe it's because of the pressure on them.

For instance, about 10 or 15 years ago, it was forbidden for men to wear a T-shirt or a short-sleeved shirt, especially in offices. They would stop you if you wore a short-sleeved shirt. But right now, no. This has changed.

I faced another problem: changing my religion. This is so dangerous. If you were born in a Christian family, this is no problem for you. But if you were a Muslim and changed your religion, this is a problem. They will kill you, put you in jail, or make lots of problems for your family – sisters, father, mother.

For this reason, lots of guys who have changed their religion have gone to other countries. Last year, when Angela Merkel opened the German borders, it was the best opportunity for them to leave the country and reach a safe land that respected their religion, their thoughts, their attitudes.

If the condition of my country was like Turkey or Malaysia, fewer people would be interested in Christianity, because they would have more options, more privacy.

People want to enjoy all the moments of their lives. If the Iranian regime continues like this, and doesn't respect people's opinions, then step by step, the regime will lose support and there will be another revolution.

People who support the regime are not ordinary people. They are those who are connected to the Ayatollahs, to the regime, by jobs and family. These people are the only ones who always support the regime. If you look at the news, you will see hundreds of demonstrators supporting the regime – they are these people. The Iranian media exaggerate their numbers.

After the 1979 revolution, the leader of the Islamic Republic at the time, the Ayatollah Khomeini, said famously that, 'We should spread our Islam to other countries.' I can tell you that most of Iran's policies today follow that pronouncement. It's not possible to do it, though; it is very difficult. They are trying in Syria, Qatar, Iraq, Bahrain, Lebanon, Sudan.

Because Iran is rich, the regime just sells the oil and spends the money in other countries, not on their citizens. Because of that, the Iranians are always un-satisfied with their government. The country is so rich, but they don't see anything of it.

If you are smart, go to Iran, and talk with people in different levels of society, you will find that the majority don't like the regime. Even our fathers and mothers, the previous generation who made the revolution, are not satisfied. This is because at the beginning of the revolution, the regime promised lots of things to the people, which they didn't do. So the people are angry and don't trust the regime. They are liars, and have lied often.

The regime has a lot of power now. After the Iran–Iraq War finished, the regime started to produce lots of weapons, some independently, some with the help of North Korea and Russia, who always supports Iran. So some politicians say Iran is maybe the most powerful country in the region.

From the outside of Iran, I can say it is impossible to change this powerful regime. And also, Iranians are patriotic. They love their land. People would even come back to Iran to support their country, if it was attacked from outside. There is just one other way in which to resist: from the inside. We have lots of opposition parties. But they have to organise outside of Iran. For example, we have seven or eight just of Kurdish parties against Iran – outside Iran, leading the movement. It's hard to send the message to inside Iran. And if the regime realises you have a connection to the outside, they imprison you.

When I was younger, as a teenager, I used to go to the libraries and read books, mostly self-help books, for instance, 'How to be rich', or 'Follow your heart', translated into Farsi. The regime didn't censor these books; they didn't think they could brainwash us. Because I knew English at that time, I could also download these books from the Internet and read them in English. I was thinking about how we can be successful and have a high standard of living. My life was ok, but I was always searching for the best lifestyle for a person. I compared the conditions of my real life in Iran with the books, and I thought that something was wrong. I should do something to change my situation, and my heart said this is not the true way – you should go another way, take another direction.

I have some relatives who lived for many years in other countries. When they visited Iran for the New Year holidays, they were always telling us about life in foreign countries. So I compared my life in Iran to what I knew from them about European countries. I researched more about these standards for living and I found that it was totally different in a European country.

Step by step, these ideas and the books had their effect on my mind. I began to dream of a perfect, free life in another country. I asked my mum what she would think if I lived in another country, married a non-Iranian woman, perhaps had another religion. She said that it would be ok; we all worship the same God.

I had a friend with whom I shared an apartment, in Teheran; he was from a Christian family. He often said things about Christianity. He was much more re-laxed than other friends – no stress! He invited me to his church and I attended some services. Then my friend left for another city. But now I was familiar with Christianity; I had the background.

Time passed. Sometimes, I read the Bible, secretly, because my friends were Muslims. I was also a Muslim, but I knew about Christianity; I was considering the differences between them. I was interested more and more in this religion. I went to a house church sometimes, in an apartment, and we talked about the Bible. This was 18 months ago.

After a while, some neighbours of the apartment grew suspicious of people coming twice a week and thought it might be a house church; they called the police. They arrested two of my friends and kept them in jail for ten days. The rest of us escaped and changed our house church, but the services were less attended because people were afraid.

The police told my friends that they and their families would face problems. Under this pressure, my friends gave them the names of all of us. One day, my cell phone was ringing with an unknown number. That was so strange for me; I thought it might be an agent of the secret police, and it was. He told me, 'Hey Majid' (already he knew my name), 'We know you are attending some house churches, and if you want to avoid problems for yourself and your family, it's better to stop that. Otherwise, you are responsible for yourself and your life.' After that time, I never attended house churches, but in my free time I read the Bible and followed some Christianity channels on satellite. I knew these guys – they were serious about what they said.

I continued my original life until last year. The government opened the borders. That was a good chance for us, for many people like me, to escape from the country and come illegally to Europe. First, I tried applying for a passport. Usually in Iran after 15–20 days, it will be ready. For me, after one month, I called them again, and they told me that 'You should come to the office.' There, they told me that 'We can't give you a passport, and we also can't say the reason, so it's better to forget this.'

Governments are often the main perpetrators of human rights violations. In many cases, such as that told by Mohammed Ahmed, governments also create divisions and urge ethnic groups to target each other.

Mohammed Ahmed (from Sudan):
My name is Mohammed Ahmed, from Sudan, Darfur district. I was born in a Jabel Marra village, and I love my village. We used to live in a good type of house; it is called a 'gotya' and is made of grass on the top side, and the bottom part is made from mud, in a round shape. We also have 'rakoba', which is also made from grass, and we use it as a hall for rest in summertime, because of the sunshine. Our life is so simple, as you know, in the village. The regular job is that of the farmer. We used to plant different types of seeds, including sorghum, semsem, Sudanese peanut, pearl millet, watermelon and okra. We do all this in the autumn season. Also, we have animal breeding, like sheep, cows and poultry farming.

The leader of the tribe we call 'sheik'. I belong to the Fur tribe to which Darfur has been given, and which belongs to it. The sheik of our tribe is my grandfather. He deserved to be our tribe leader; he used to help the people and solve all the problems among them, whatever the problem was. I am so proud of him, and proud to be his grandson. All these years, we were staying safely, and everything was pretty cool.

In 2003, the government started to sow problems among the tribes in Darfur which are called the regional tribes. I think that they succeeded in doing that, and then the tribes started to dislike and fight each other. Especially the ethnic Arabs disliked people of Black ethnicity – and I belong to the Black people – because the government told them Sudan belongs to the Arabs. But it does not, and history knows that Sudan belongs to the Black people, and everybody around the world knows that. The Arabs came to the Sudan through trade, from the Arabian Peninsula.

So then the Arabs started killing Black people, especially in Darfur, and raping people, for no reason. The people who are killing and raping are a group of Arabs who used to live in and around our villages. They are not that much stronger than our people, but they have been mobilised by and supported by the government with weapons and cars, materially and morally, to kill us. Therefore they killed and raped and burned our villages and stole everything, and they replaced us.

Now, most of the people are in Kalma camp which is the biggest camp in Darfur; it is in South Darfur – Nyala. Other people are in the Abu Shouk camp in North Darfur – Al Fasher. Now these people are still suffering from health, food and even water problems. There is no education and even no safe place. There are diseases, people are dying every single day, and there is not any cure. People are suffering from everything, and famine too. There is no organisation to help these people at all. There were a few organisations, but the government did not allow them to help these people.

I feel so bad for my people. I hope I can help them in this situation.

The government is targeting students at the university, especially those who come from Darfur, generally Black people, and arresting and torturing them. Some get released and the others, they get killed. The reason is that we have some people in Darfur who became the opposition. They are in the bush and are still rising up against the government to protect our people and change the regime, which committed a lot of crimes against the community, and genocide. I hope peace comes to Sudan, to let the people live in safety.

Because of our people who are rising up and trying to protect our people, the government thinks the students are also part of the opposition. That is why they are arresting and killing them. I saw all these things happening, and I told my father about leaving Sudan, and he said that 'If you don't leave, they may kill you too, the same as happened to the other people.' He helped me with some money to travel to Libya.

The absence of democracy and freedom at home makes the current situation in which the authors find themselves, even more absurd. People who have escaped state oppression, torture, detention and lack of basic rights have ended up in the middle of Europe, struggling for the rights that they thought they would not achieve back home but that could be guaranteed here. There seems to be no hope, not back home, not in the new life the authors were supposed to reach in Europe. Perhaps, if we can continue to see humanity around us and appreciate it, we will have hope.

FIGURE I.2
*A game of football with, on the other side, a game of cricket.
Photo by Teddy (from Eritrea).*

Teddy (from Eritrea):
I was previously working in South Sudan as a nurse for MSF [Médecins sans Frontières]. Wherever you go in the world, you see the Eritrean diaspora: South Sudan, North Sudan, Uganda, even Kenya, as well as Europe and North America.

I hate politics. Bad things happen to your family and your friends because of politics. In Africa, there is the same issue of dictatorship and corruption without human rights, everywhere.

We are supporting the opposition democratic parties, but they cannot hold meetings. When you are free, you can chat with your friends or use social media. In Eritrea, you are afraid to say political things, even on Facebook.

In the 'Jungle', people of different nationalities play football and cricket together. I don't play cricket but I like to watch it. It's a favourite game of Afghanis.

In Eritrea, wherever you go, people do running and also bicycling, which is the favourite sport.

When you see a good footballer, you watch and appreciate them. You hate the bad administration of your country. When you hate everything, you have lost your hope.

CHAPTER 2

Journeys

Introduction

The dangerous and circuitous journeys undertaken by migrants and refugees to reach the so-called 'haven' of Europe have been documented at length since the summer of 2015 – broadcast over 24-hour rolling news coverage and social media platforms, replete with bold red arrows showing the trajectories of migrants and refugees from across Asia and Africa as they converge on Europe. However, this version of journeys undertaken often fails to acknowledge the ways in which refugees are held up and forced to find more dangerous alternatives. It conceals the people and organisations responsible for the life-threatening conditions under which refugees move across into Europe. Over the course of the first eight months of 2016, the number of people who reached European shores via journeys across either the Mediterranean or the Aegean Seas stood at over 268,000.

While sanctuary from conflict and persecution is often found in neighbouring countries – 86 per cent of all refugees are located in the Global South – finding social, economic and political security for the displaced is not guaranteed. This chapter draws attention to this shortfall, which propels refugees on to more journeys. The accounts that follow describe some of the constraints which refugees face. The authors vividly describe the exposure to continued violence and risk of life that confronts them on their journeys.

Evading authority

We begin this chapter with an account from Africa. As we heard in the previous chapter, Africa had been detained and tortured by the security services in his home country on account of his record for organising his local community. On his release, his brother urged him to seek refuge in a neighbouring country.

> *Africa (from Sudan):*
> I chose to go to Libya. It took three months. In Libya, I started to fight many fights. You can fight the police – they took your money, took your phone. Anything in your pocket, they took it by force.
> That was in 2015. This is the kindliness of Libya – they clean you out. After that, there was nothing to do but to get out. After being out on the streets – there was no other way. I thought the best thing for me would be to go to Egypt – it would be better there.

Africa's vulnerability as an asylum seeker to figures of authority, particularly the police is not uncommon. Refugees and migrants are often singled out as being a nuisance, or categorised as deviant by state officials. The lack of protection afforded to them in countries of first refuge leaves them particularly open to mistreatment by officials. For African migrants and refugees, there is also the spectre of racism to contend with.

Mohammed Ahmed (from Sudan):

I travelled to Libya by car through the desert for 15 days; then we reached Libya. We tried to find out how to get a job, and then we got a job, but the country is not safe and does not have a government. It just has militias and rebels. Sometimes when they see you on the street, especially when you are Black, then they stop you and check your pockets, and take all that you have got, and they tell you, 'We don't want to see you again in these places.' Sometimes, when you go to work, after you did your work, they just tell you that 'We don't have money for it.' If you talk, they just kill you for no reason. And also, they call Black people slaves.

This leaves many refugees and migrants wary of interaction with figures of authority. Strategies are devised in order to minimise possibilities of encounter but are ultimately unsustainable, as we shall see with the account of Ali Bajdar.

For Ali Bajdar, the fact of his village being Kurdish was enough for him to evacuate his home on hearing news of the approach of Daesh[1] – as we read in the last chapter. Initially, Ali Bajdar was displaced to a refugee camp on the Iraqi side of the border with Turkey. In the ensuing panic to reach safety, he lost contact with his elderly mother. In the camp, he searched in vain for his mother. To this day, he has had no news of her whereabouts. Here is Ali Bajdar describing the next stage of his journey:

---

1 Since the American occupation of Iraq – security swings to and fro between militias and armed groups far from the political centre of Baghdad. Residents of small towns and villages caught between the cross-hairs of the naked political ambition of these groups now find themselves held ransom to their ethnic or religious affiliation.

Ali Bajdar (from Iraq):

My uncle helped me to get to Turkey and he travelled with me. He wanted to help me because he knew I was sick. I didn't have any money so he paid for my travel. We went by car and at times we had to walk. He didn't stay with me when we reached Turkey. He told me to go to a house in a village where there would be an old lady waiting for me. She would help me and provide me with food. She cooked me food. She was nice and almost like a mother to me. She knew about my bad health and she helped me with everything. I miss her.

Before my uncle left, he told me I wasn't allowed to leave the house. If the police saw me, they would put me in prison because I don't have a passport or any ID card. I could go out for ten minutes, that was it, and I always had to stay around the house. A few times, my uncle came to visit me. I stayed for 14 months in Turkey but health care is very expensive there, so eventually I had to leave.

I don't think I will ever go back to Turkey. Imagine if I told people in Turkey that I am Kurdish. They'd ask me what I was doing there, if I was studying or working. I don't have a passport, and could probably go to prison because of that. Because of the civil war between the Turks and the Kurds, it isn't a good place for me to be.

I left six months ago. We were a group of people travelling together of whom I didn't know anyone except for my uncle, who had paid for the journey and travelled with me. Sometimes we walked, sometimes we went by car and at other times by train. In Germany my uncle and I got separated from one another – we lost one another. One night the police came. People tried to avoid the police and went in different directions. I couldn't find my uncle again after that. The smuggler told me, that we had to keep on travelling, and that my uncle would reach us again eventually. Now I don't know how to find him again. Maybe he has changed his name. While I was travelling, my stomach was causing me so much pain that there were times when I had to stay behind and wait until I was able to travel again. I still have pain.

Ali Bajdar's account also illustrates the stop-start nature of these journeys. It tells of loved ones who fall by the wayside – of journeys not completed. For many, this is characterised by slippages in time where movement is restricted and constrained to avoid interaction with the violence of police authority or by actual detention.

Shaheen (from Afghanistan):
The first country which I crossed, that was Iran. The cruellest police in the world are Iranian police. When Afghans cross the border, they shoot people. I saw them shoot people in front of my eyes. We couldn't even stop for the dead people. The guy told us, 'If you stop for them, they'll shoot you, like them.' I walked for three days without food – there was some water; we just carried the water in our bags. I faced a lot of problems on this border.

During the height of the 2015 spontaneous movement of refugees into and across Europe, negotiating the border from a state outside of the Schengen area back into Europe meant that evading border surveillance was a lot more haphazard, and subject to good fortune.

Majid (from Iran):
On the other side of the border, some Serbian soldiers pointed at a far light and told us, 'You know, that place is the border of Croatia. You just have to walk there in a straight line. Croatian border soldiers are waiting to process you.' At first sight, it seemed very close, but we walked for more than half an hour. The ground was very muddy and icy. At the border, there was one big tent. They searched us – a quick search. In two different lines, they made fingerprints. They were so busy, looking at papers that I just crossed quickly, without fingerprinting. Those guys who got fingerprinted faced lots of problems later. Just three of us five didn't get fingerprinted.

Shaheen writes about an encounter with Bulgarian police. Shaheen and his fellow travellers had been previously warned by a smuggler that the Bulgarian police had a reputation for being severe. Eager to continue their onward journey and reluctant to prolong their stay in Greece, Shaheen and a group of 17 refugees and four smugglers crossed into Bulgaria.

Shaheen (from Afghanistan):
At first light, the agents said we should leave this place. We walked for an hour. Suddenly, someone fired on us. When we ran, they shouted at us, 'Don't run! We will shoot you; just stay where you are.' But the agents said, 'Run!', so we ran. The Bulgarian police started firing.

FIGURE 2.1
Graffiti on wall outside of Moria Camp, Lesvos, Greece.
December 2015. Photo by Tahir Zaman.

We ran faster; then we lost each other, but my friend
and I stayed together. We ran for 30 minutes. After a
while, we got tired, and stopped running. Suddenly, I
heard the sound of dogs. I told my friend, 'They've set
the dogs on us; now they'll catch us – no need to keep
running.' We decided to climb a tree to hide from the
dogs. After some minutes, I saw the dogs were down
at the bottom of the tree and they were barking in our
direction. That was a very hard time for us. The dogs
were dangerous and big. I shouted to my friend, 'Don't
be afraid, they can't climb up the tree, stay where you
are!' Eventually, the police reached us. They pointed
guns towards us and said, 'Come down', in English.
Feeling relieved. I said in my heart, 'Oh good, they
know English.' Again he said, 'Come down.' I replied,
'The dogs will bite us.' Again he said, 'Come down, or
I will shoot you.' I had heard about these Bulgarian

police; they are very cruel. Maybe they would shoot me. So we decided to come down.

When I was a step away from the ground, then they set the dogs free, and the dogs started attacking us, biting us. I covered my face, and shouted, 'Please stop the dogs, I'll never come this way again.' And I never did come again, the dogs bit me too much.

Finally, one of their commanders gave orders to call off the dogs. He started asking me questions; he spoke good English. 'Why are you coming to Europe? We don't want you; we hate you people; don't come here.' I said, crying, 'I want to save my life; my life was in great danger.' For a while, he just looked at my face. I thought, 'Maybe he has a soft heart and he'll leave us be.' Then he said, in a cruel tone, 'Now I will show you how to save your life.' Oh my God. He started kicking me with his big, hard army boots; he wanted to break my bones. Eventually he beat me so much, he broke two of my fingers on the spot. I saw some other boys; they were also bleeding.

Then they took us and put us in a police van. They drove us to the army base and put us in a very dirty room. The temperature was cold there, and there was nothing to wear or sleep on; it was an empty room. One of the army officers came and said, 'You are Muslims.' We said, 'Yes.' He said, 'We are keeping you here in this room, pigs.'

That was a very hard time for us. They kept us for two days, asking us, 'Where are the other boys?' At that time, we were just eight boys, and we didn't know about the others, where they were, because we had lost each other. After two days, they released us in some woodland. They said, 'This is the way to a Turkish forest – go back to Turkey, never come back or we will shoot you.' So together, we ran. After an hour, we got tired and we just walked. We walked for the whole day.

Eventually, we reached the Turkish border. We crossed the border and reached a village. Some people there saw that we were in a very bad condition. Then suddenly, we saw some Turkish police vans coming towards us. They arrested us and started searching us. They asked, 'Why are you hurt so much?' We told them that the Bulgarian police had set dogs on to us. The Turkish police officer talked with his superior, and told him that 'We arrested some boys; they are very seriously injured.' He told the hospital, 'Look, I am coming', so when we reached the hospital, there were lots of people there and some doctors waiting for us. They started treating us, and the police questioned us. I told them the whole story. They treated us well. After some days, they gave us a paper, like a visa, for three months, then left us in Istanbul.

Recalibrating journeys

The crossing of the border from the country of origin does not necessarily dictate that the refugee finds herself bereft of all capacity and resources. On either side of a border it is not uncommon to find people belonging to the same religious and ethnic affiliation, speaking the same language, or even perhaps being part of a wider kinship group. This allows refugees to negotiate their exile more evenly and on their own terms. However, when the overall security

situation begins to worsen as it did for Muhammad, a
Syrian Kurdish refugee in the eastern provinces of Turkey
in the dying days of the summer of 2015, onward migration
beckoned once more.

Muhammad (from Syria):
I'll tell you the story. To go from Diyarbakir to Izmir,
alone in the night, I left my house, of which I had
precious memories with my small family and kind
friends. I still remember the moment when I closed
the door behind me. It made me recall all the memories of when I left my home in Kobanî and couldn't go
back again, and all the happy days in this small town
of Diyarbakir. Everything will disappear once again.
How many houses will I have to build in order to have
a stable life?

Firstly, I didn't want to travel to Europe. I had a good
life in Turkey. But my brother, who was in Germany,
insisted I should come, for my sister; she didn't want
to travel if I didn't. I had to persuade her to leave. She
and her husband were in danger in Turkey. In the end,
I departed with two of my sisters and their families
(kids and husbands). They left just when I decided
also to come with them. None of them were in a safe
state in Turkey. And for me too, it seemed Turkey
wouldn't be a safe place for very long. And there's no
good future for my specialism in Turkey.

So before I travelled, I decided that I'd help my
family reach Greece. Then they'd complete the journey
to Germany by themselves; it was safe that time.

Decisions on where to go are often fluid. Information is passed back and forth between others undertaking similar journeys.

> *Zeeshan Javid (from Pakistan):*
> We left Pakistan on the 28th of March. We went from Pakistan to Iran, from Iran to Istanbul, Istanbul to Bulgaria and Hungary, then to Serbia and after that Italy. My cousin was going to Germany and I went to Belgium. We separated because if conditions in Germany were good I would come there and if conditions in Belgium were good he would come and meet me there. I left Belgium and he left Germany, and we went to Calais, arriving in July. It was a very bad time. We were also fingerprinted in Bulgaria.

When faced with indefinite disruptions to how they imagined their journey would unfold, refugees turn to people who best know how to navigate their way beyond increasingly complex border crossings: smugglers. The following accounts of authors describe more vividly the degree to which their journeys had been beholden to networks of smugglers – mapping varied and everchanging routes into Europe. For some, remembering the events along the journey were difficult to retell – and they preferred to gloss over the details – such as Shikeb, whose experience of the journey had been traumatic to the point where it was better to forget.

> *Shikeb (from Afghanistan):*
> This is the first time I have left Afghanistan. I don't

find it interesting to go to another country. I want to live with my mum forever. I came first to Iran, on a flight, then to Turkey, then Bulgaria. It took a long time – I don't remember, I think six months. I made my life in Afghanistan; then they wanted to kill me. Why didn't they kill me the first time, when they killed my father?

Following Shaheen's aborted attempt to cross into Europe through Bulgaria, he found himself back in Turkey and in contact with his 'migration agent', or smuggler.

Shaheen (from Afghanistan):
Again, we called our agent, so he sent a man to pick us up. After a few days, when we were feeling better, the agent asked us, 'Which way do you want to select again, by foot or by sea?' We said, 'By sea, but we have one request.' He asked, 'What is your request?' 'We will pay you more money for just one boat for us five boys.' He said, 'You have to pay me €500 each', so we accepted. Then he said, 'You have to buy life jackets for yourselves.' We bought the life jackets.

At ten o'clock, they took us to a city by the name of Izmir. At last, they brought the dinghy for us. The agent told us, 'I've checked the Internet tonight and the sea is very quiet, so you can go more easily', and he showed us again a light, very far off. Then we started the journey …

After two days, a Greek agent arrived and he gave some money to the shepherd, he brought some clothes for us … Then he said, 'Be ready for the night, I am going to bring ship tickets to Athens.' So at last he made some documents for us, we bought the tickets, and we started on our journey towards Athens, the capital of Greece, in a big ship such as I had never seen in my whole life.

After some hours, we reached Athens. There was a man waiting for us at the harbour. We found the man, and he took us to his home. It was a very beautiful house. He kept us there for some days. After that, he said, 'Tomorrow we will go towards the Macedonian border.' He took us towards the border, and after four or five hours, we reached it. When we got to the border, there were lots of people there who had been staying there for days. Crossing the border was very hard because a lot of police were there with guns and tear gas.

We stayed there; some volunteers gave us a tent, so we pitched the tent there at the side, because we were very tired, and we rested for some hours. After that time, some people started shouting, 'Open the border, Open the border!' So we woke up. We saw that people were rushing at the police, trying to cross the border. At last, clashes broke out between refugees and police. The police used tear gas, and there were children and women there also. Everyone started running a little further away from the border.

These things continued happening for some days. We called the agent, 'It is not possible to cross the border.' He told us, 'I'm sending a man' he had taken from another route. After some hours, a man came, and said, 'We'll go by the forest; it is about ten hours away by foot.' So we accepted. Then we started walking. We walked for the whole night. By about sunrise, we reached Macedonia. Then we stopped in the woods by the road, and the agent called his friend to come with a car. He took us to a big farmhouse; we stayed there for some days.

From there, we moved towards the Serbian border. The weather was very cold and wet. We started walking; all of our clothes were wet and soaked right through. We walked like this for two nights and three days, in very bad conditions. We were tired, and some boys were sick. Eventually, we reached a Serbian border city. We went to a bus stop and we waited for the bus.

Suddenly, two or three police vans came and arrested us all. They took us to the police station and took our fingerprints. They then took us back to the bus stop and loaded us onto a big bus. There were about forty of us in all. Then the driver took us to Belgrade, the capital of Serbia. Six hours later, we reached Belgrade. Eventually we found a park there, by the name of 'Afghan Park'. When we reached the park, there were lots of people there, and we were very hungry. Some people brought food and some water for us. Then I asked someone to lend me a mobile, and I called my agent. I told him that I was in Serbia. He said, 'Stay with the person with the phone, I am sending someone to fetch you.' After 20 minutes, someone called and asked my name. I talked with him, and gave him the location of my whereabouts. After a few hours, he came and took me to his home. I stayed there for several days.

Encountering smugglers

Unable to fly into Europe as a result of tough European migration policies, those seeking security are forced into the embrace of migration agents. For some authors, smugglers were facilitators who made journeys possible that otherwise would have been nearly impossible to undertake. Majid explains how smugglers facilitated movement from different staging posts of his long journey to Calais.

Majid (from Iran):
I arranged to go to Romia city, near the border with Turkey. I had heard that it was easier to go from there to Turkey illegally, with the help of smugglers. I talked to one of them and paid him to help me cross. After two nights staying at his shelter, at midnight, we went to the Turkish border – 21 of us – Iranians, Pakistanis, Afghans and Iraqis. We were so lucky that there were no families with us, because it was a difficult route and we had to keep quiet; we were all men. We had to climb a mountain for seven hours: very difficult, steep climbing. In the middle of this, after about three-and-a-half hours, suddenly we heard shooting. All of us lay down. The Iranian military shot for over a minute near us, but fortunately, none of us were injured.

After seven hours' hard climbing, we neared the top of the mountain. Our smuggler told us, 'It's better to sit down here and be quiet, because we are very close to the Turkish border.' Two of them left us, going 50 metres closer, to check the situation of the Turkish soldiers patrolling at the border. After half an hour, they came back and told us, 'It's a good time.' They commanded us, 'You should run so fast, as fast as possible, immediately!' All of us ran down the other side of the steep and stony hill. After about ten minutes, we reached the woods at the end of the slope, and continued running. After 20 minutes, our smugglers said, 'You can rest here; we have crossed the border and we are now in Turkey.'

We rested for just ten minutes, and continued, jogging straight ahead, over three or four smaller hills, until we reached a very small village. Our smuggler placed us in a tiny shelter and told us, 'It's best to rest here and be ready when I come back with a car.' We rested, drank water and ate some biscuits and whatever we had in our backpacks. We shared between us whatever we had. Some guys didn't have anything, not even a backpack. After around two hours, the smuggler came back with a small van, and we got in, to go to Istanbul. There, we stayed for one day in an apartment that the smuggler had. They fed us very delicious food. This smuggler was really a very kind guy.

The next night, we took another van, to go to Çanakkale, one of the nearest cities to Greece. This time, our guy called another smuggler to take us. When we reached the city, that guy placed us all in a very old house and said, 'Wait, and be ready!' We waited there four or five hours until he came back with three Turkish taxis and told us, 'Get in the taxis immediately!' We were going to the border point – the last place in Turkey.

The taxi drivers drove at high speed; I saw the speedometer: 140km an hour. After 45 minutes, we reached the border. The driver opened the door and said, 'Go under the trees, right away!' We ran, reached the trees and lay down under them. I remember that they were olive trees – the kind that produce what is, in Iran, a high quality and expensive oil. It was evening; it was getting dark. That night, we couldn't get on the boat because, our smuggler told us, police patrols were checking, so he wouldn't try to bring the boat by road.

The next day, two families joined us. On the evening of that day, unfortunately we again didn't get on the boat, because the smuggler told us that the priority was moving the families. They put the families and some other new individuals – six or seven – into a boat, started the motors, and it set off for Greece. So we slept there for the second night.

The day after, around four in the afternoon, some police approached the trees, and we had to run away. After two hours waiting far away from our first location, the police left and we came back underneath the trees. At about seven in the evening, our smuggler brought a big inflatable boat, 11 or 12 metres long, of the kind the Iranian military might use. He forced us to inflate it, with the help of some pumps. After around 50 minutes, we finished, and the boat was ready. He told us, 'Just be relaxed, teenagers should get in first, and that guy (he pointed to someone), he is your navigator.'

They forced us to carry the boat to the shore; it was so heavy, because they had already attached the engine. Quickly, the teenagers got in, and then the rest of us. At the last moment, the smuggler told the navigator, 'Look, see that light? Just go straight – that's a Greek island. And don't be afraid of the Turkish coastguard!'

77

So we headed to Greece. In the middle of the journey, a military Turkish coastguard ship stopped in front of us, and with the help of a loudspeaker told us, 'Stop, and go back to Turkey!' This time was so scary. We were sure they would never fire on us, but we might fail in our dream of reaching Europe. Many Muslims among us were praying.

Our navigator didn't care about the coastguard. He was a brave man. He turned to the right of the ship – he had experience of driving motorboats – and passed it. The ship turned around and came in front of us again. For the second time, they commanded us to stop, and aimed a water cannon at our boat to try to force us. But again, the navigator didn't care, continued on his way, and passed the ship again. The ship went slowly back to the Turkish side, and we were so happy. Maybe this had happened because our navigator was so brave, or because of prayer, or because God was on our side, or because our dreams were so powerful, or all of these things!

In stark contrast, Shaheen recalls the unscrupulous character of the smugglers he encountered:

Shaheen (from Afghanistan):
At last we reached Teheran, the capital of Iran. I stayed for two days there. Then they put us in a container. We were 85 people in the container, and the weather was very hot. The Iranian agent told us they would put on the air conditioning in the container, so they closed the doors and then sealed up the doors from the outside.

We moved towards the Turkish border. The agent told us that the journey would take ten hours. They put the air conditioning on in the container and after two hours they switched off the air conditioner. Within ten minutes, we got problems taking breaths. We were beating the container, but the driver was not hearing the sounds, so we all started crying and shouting. People were saying, 'I am dying, I am dying.' At that time, I was thinking that this was the last movement of my life. My children and my wife were just circling before my eyes. I could hear my little daughter just telling me, 'Dad, don't go, please don't leave us.'

At last tears came from my eyes, I couldn't stop myself. So I cried so much and sweated because the weather was too hot. Sweat soaked through my clothes and I ended up taking everything off except my underwear. So suddenly I saw my mobile phone which was switched off because in the start the agent told us to 'Switch off your mobile because it will be traced by Iranian police when we're crossing.' So this was my last time to do something, and I was going to do anything to save 84 lives and myself. I switched on my mobile phone but for some time there was no signal. I tried so many times. Eventually, it worked and I called my agent in Afghanistan and just told him that 'we are dying, 85 persons in a container', but I couldn't explain everything, just told him to call the Iranian agent to call the driver. So after five minutes, the driver stopped the truck and there was a small window in the back of container. He opened that window so all these 85 persons rushed to the window for taking breath. That was a small window and they covered up all the window again, and they left all the children and women in the back. When they did this, I shouted at them, 'If you do like this, all these children and women will die except us. So please let the window stay down and open and oxygen will come so we can all breathe well.' So, thanks be to God, they accepted, and everybody sat down, and after five minutes the breathing was normal.

After a while, we reached near to the Turkish border and the container stopped at the side of the road. After 20 minutes, the driver opened the door, and he said, 'Come down, hurry up, hurry up!' That was around ten o'clock at night. He said, 'Stay together at the side of the road.' We had been sitting there for a while when I saw four men coming toward us. As they approached, one of them just started counting, and he said, 'How many are you?' We said, '85 people', so he started swearing at us in Farsi, for no good reason – because he wanted to put pressure on us. We started walking. After four hours, we reached near to a mountain top. He said, 'We have 15 minutes' break – after that, we have to climb up the mountain.' That was a very high mountain. We started climbing. I saw the women and children and that the agent was shouting at them. But they couldn't climb like us. Suddenly, the agent pointed a gun and he said, 'Because of you people I can't stay.'

So we, some boys and I, decided to help these women and children. I had one baby with a small bag; so we divided them. So with difficulty, we reached the top of the mountain. We took a short break there. After that, we started our descent; that was very hard.

Suddenly, some people started shouting. I said, 'what's wrong?' Someone said, 'A guy's fallen off the mountain.' So I told the agent in Farsi, 'The man has fallen down.' He said, 'Forget about him.' I said, 'Why? He was our friend.' Suddenly he pointed the gun towards me, and he snarled, 'You want me to throw you down like him? JUST WALK!' I was scared, and I stayed back. At long last, we came down to some houses. They put us in a barn where you'd put sheep, goats and other animals. We stayed there for three days. They gave us a few pieces of bread and very little water.

After three days, they brought four cars and they put in each 21 people except in one, they put 22 people. We moved towards the last part of the Turkish border crossing. They had put 21 people in a small car so that time was very hard for us. They drove us for two hours. They were driving so fast; I don't think I've ever seen fast driving like this on a rough road. After two hours, they dropped us in a place like a desert. We stayed there for a while. When it was dark, they said, 'Now move on.' The night was very dark; I couldn't even see a man walking in front of me, we just held onto each other's bags. So then the agent said, 'Are you ready?' We said, 'Yes.' And he said, 'If anyone is left on the way, I can't stop for him. If anyone gets tired, we can't wait for him; I'll leave him for animals. We should walk fast before it is sunrise, so be quick.' I said a prayer silently, 'O my God help me for the sake of my small daughter, and for the sake of my old parents.' So I started listing the names of all my family members, one by one. I ended up crying to myself. I told myself 'what kind of situation are you in? If you don't walk, they'll leave you here.' I gave myself a final push. And I started walking.

Eritrea provides an account which draws attention to the exploitative African smuggling networks on which many refugees, for lack of safe and regular means to cross borders, are dependent upon to reach Europe.

Eritrea (from Eritrea):
I remember we had a two days' journey to reach Sudan. We spent two days on foot to the border and then I stayed in Khartoum for about twenty days.

I remember I was sick, maybe it was because of hunger and thirst. I didn't have any other options than to leave Sudan, pass the desert to go to Europe. It is not safe to stay in Sudan. There is a link between the Sudanese and Eritrean governments so if soldiers in Sudan catch you, you are sent back to Eritrea and might end up in prison forever. We were afraid of that and that's why I immediately left Sudan to go to Libya. I had to pay a large amount of money for the journey.

I had a cousin in Sudan and I stayed with him for the twenty days. During that time, I didn't leave the house. I took the opportunity to study for my IELTS [International English Language Testing System] exams so that I would be qualified in English. My brother in Israel and my uncle in America helped me financially to leave Sudan and go ahead with my journey. I started my journey while I was still sick, but it wasn't an option to wait.

The journey started in the Sahara. In the desert there were many evil things that you would rather be without. The smugglers are not good people. They are very cruel people, especially towards the ladies. We saw many evil things happening to the ladies. The smugglers liked to have sex with them. It was against their will; it happened by force. They were very cruel towards them.

The Sahara is not a comfortable place. It took us about two days to reach the Libyan border by truck. We faced many challenges because we did not have enough water and food with us. There was no option; we had to resist the hunger and thirst.

The Libyans accepted us at the border. We were loaded onto trucks. There were about four trucks and I got on the first one. It was a four-hour drive to the place we were going. The driver was driving fast and we told him to slow down. We were on a hill and suddenly our driver slammed on the brakes because he realised it could be dangerous, and moved the truck away from the path immediately. Another truck was right behind us because our driver was leading the way. The car behind us slipped down the hill, it fell down maybe twenty metres. There were about 25 people in the truck. 'Is this reality?' I thought. It was like being in a movie. I was in shock. There were ladies and even a six-month-old child in the car. God is good. Only four of the people died. I see such things in Hollywood films so I was really surprised at that moment. There weren't any nurses or doctors and many were injured. We didn't have any other option than to continue our journey.

One day we reached the destination: Ajdabiya. The smugglers did not care about the bodies. They might have buried them, I don't know. They were hitting us and they shouted at us; it was very terrifying. I remember thinking, 'Why am I doing this to myself? I have no other option, what can I do?' I argued with myself, with my soul, but there was no other option. We stayed in Ajdabiya for one week without enough food, without clean water, without washing ourselves. It was terrifying. I don't know how we made it through that week.

Thank you Lord, after one week we left and arrived in the coast area of Tripoli. On the way, we passed through a city where ISIS were. We saw their flags. We were afraid of them. The smugglers told us: 'If you speak too loud, ISIS will come and murder you. You have to stay silent.' They kept us inside a big truck. They used bricks and wood to construct a lorry that looked as if it was carrying a load, where we could stay inside. It was very hot, especially for the ladies and their babies. The babies were crying. We didn't have an option. If ISIS had heard us, we would not have been here today.

Thank God we reached Tripoli's coast area. After staying at the coast without food and water for about one week, we had dehydrated our bodies and many people were suffering from diarrhoea and typhoid, and there was a lot of itching. When I remember that scene, I don't have words to explain it. I can say it was a kind of hell.

Then we continued our journey crossing the Mediterranean Sea. If you didn't have the money to pay for the further journey, you'd have to stay in that hell. I paid money and was therefore able to leave. The boat wasn't really a boat and it wasn't a ship. It was made of wood. The smugglers don't care about safety, they care about their money. About 700 people were kept in a boat capable of carrying 400 people, and I was downstairs. It's the worst place to be. If you're upstairs, there is a good temperature and a good wind – it's comfortable to breathe. If there's any danger, those who are downstairs cannot be saved. Those who are upstairs have better chances. If people came to rescue us, they'd save the ones upstairs first.

We spent eleven hours on the boat until the Italian Navy came to rescue us. There was a big sort of misunderstanding. Some of the people wanted to get off the boat immediately and get on the Italian Navy's ship. The weight on the ship wasn't balanced. The Navy was shouting to us that if we didn't keep it balanced we'd turn upside down. This didn't happen, thanks to the wisdom of the Navy. They brought one ship at each side of the boat and helped to balance the boat. Then slowly we were transferred to their big ship. It took one night and six hours to reach Sicily. The Italian ship had come a long way to help people. Many would have died if it wasn't for the help the Europeans give the people coming from Africa crossing the sea.

Milkesa similarly describes his difficult time at the hands of smugglers and Egyptian authorities. Countries through which refugees pass through, such as Egypt or Libya, offer little in the way of protection and assistance for refugees and forced migrants – preferring instead to encourage onward migration elsewhere. In providing little in the way of formal channels to help secure refuge, people like Milkesa are once again subjected to the whims and caprice of smugglers.

Milkesa (from Ethiopia):

I finally escaped from prison in December 2012 with the help of my aunt's husband, who bribed the prison officer. He then took me to another town in Oromio region where he hid me at his friend's house. He then arranged my safe and clandestine departure from Ethiopia, using a smuggler. I crossed into Sudanese territory on 27 December 2012, on foot, at around midnight. In Sudan, the smugglers put me and others into a car and drove us to al-Qadarif. I arrived in Khartoum on 31 December 2012, seeking sanctuary.

Once I arrived in Khartoum, my Sudanese smuggler connected me with an Oromo person named Abu Melki, who advised me to cross to Egypt. I spent five months in Khartoum, hiding myself in Abu Melki's house. He told me that there were many Oromo persons who were caught and deported to Ethiopia against their will.

Using smugglers again, I left Khartoum illegally by land on 2 May 2013, with other migrants. The smugglers detained me for more than three weeks in the Nubian Desert, asking me to pay $15,000 as a ransom or to lose one of my kidneys as compensation. At the crack of dawn on 31 May, unbelievably, one of the Eritrean detainees among the migrants took the smugglers' car's key. He confided to us that the guard was taking a nap. I and some other immigrants who swiftly boarded the car escaped in the blink of an eye, entered Aswan town in Egypt and finally arrived in Cairo.

I was registered with the regional UNHCR office in Cairo in June 2013. I was being pursued by the clandestine network of the human traffickers who had sneaked me from Sudan into Egypt. I faced random physical attack and harassment via my mobile phone. I reported this to the UNHCR office and the Egyptian police, but there was no prospect for any durable solution from the UNHCR or the police. In addition, the Egyptians saw me as a person from a hostile country, because of the Nile River dam that is being built on the Nile in Ethiopia. The Nile River is a backbone for Egypt's economy. So I became a constant target in Egypt.

The Egyptian government's laws allow refugees neither to resettle nor to work in Egypt. Hence I needed legal protection. But I didn't have an offer of resettlement from the UNHCR or any other governmental and nongovernmental organisations. As a last option, I came to Europe to ask for asylum, and to enjoy peace, freedom, security and human dignity.

Landfall in Europe

Arrival in Europe means being exposed to a dizzying array of people wanting to help. Movement from one country to the next is accompanied with varied responses from the state, local NGOs and charities, faith networks, and local residents. Here Majid talks us through the European leg of his journey:

Majid (from Iran):
We came close to the island [Lesvos] and saw one boat approaching us. The people on it said, 'We are not police, we're just volunteers, don't worry, just be relaxed. After we reach the beach, let the teenagers out

first.' At that time, I wished I was a teenager! They accompanied us to the beach, where there were many volunteers. They gave foil blankets to people who were wet, and gave us all water – 'natural mineral water' bottles. They told us, 'There is a temporary camp about a half-hour's walk away at the top of the road. When you reach it, they'll provide you with food and other necessary things, and will transfer you to the secondary camp which is necessary for you.'

At the beach, we took memorial photos with our friends, because these were our first moments in Europe. Just five of us friends, out of the 21, continued on together. We walked a steep route to the first camp, at the top. There, they served us coffee, tea and sandwiches, gave us clothes and whatever else we needed, and gave out numbers so that we could get on a bus that would transfer us to the second camp. We waited three hours, and changed some of our clothes. Then they called us, according to number, and we got on a bus to transfer.

But at the second camp, when we arrived, they told us, 'Sorry, we haven't enough space, and you will have to stay here, outside, at night so that you can get in to queue tomorrow in order to go to the third camp. Every day, we allow just a few people to go to that camp for UN registration. The bad news is we have no food, blankets – nothing.' They just gave us three or four biscuits and told us to stay till morning. When some guys left, there would be places.

The five of us consulted each other and made a new decision, to leave that camp immediately, that night, because it had no facilities. There were three local people using their cars as taxis; it was an opportunity for them. We paid them €70 to drive us a very short distance to the third and final registration camp. When we reached it and got out of the taxi, we were shocked, because we saw a very long line, about 200 metres. It was 3 or 4am. Some guys told us that 'You will have to wait here at least three or four days to register.' We talked with each other and made a decision to go in line immediately. We even ate our food, some things that we still had in our backpacks, in the line.

At 8am, they began to process, and the line moved forward. But by 3pm we had only progressed about 50m because some guys were always cheating, coming into the line with the help of their friends. We were so hungry. One of us went out of the line to find some food, because we had heard that the camp officials would distribute food – but there would not be enough. After an hour, he came back with five packs of spaghetti and we ate them in the line – just cooked spaghetti, no sauce or anything.

At 5pm, they stopped processing again, and the officials left, but we had to stay in the line. This was one of the hardest times in the journey. There were so many refugees wanting to register with the UN. By 9 or 10pm, we were so tired, we sat on our rucksacks, and went to sleep like that. There was no room in the line to lie down; people were packed together. Some guys had nothing and were just sitting on the ground and sleeping.

To the sound of loud voices, we woke up in the night and saw that there was fighting, and the line had totally vanished. After about twenty minutes, the guys made another line. We were at the end of the line again, and it was now 250 metres long.

The next morning, the officials found out that there had been fighting because of the line, so they hired some more people to process our applications. Fortunately, now, the line was moving quickly. Finally, by evening, we could register with the UN. The official told us that 'You have to go to Athens, but the only worry is buying a ticket and going there by ferry.' So we went to the other side of the small island where there were shops to buy ferry tickets. We entered the travel agency and requested the tickets. But the girl told us, 'Sorry, tickets are finished, and you should wait for tomorrow.' We had to stay near the port that night. It was cold; we bought two blankets from a local person who had them for sale, and went to sleep near the harbour. Next morning, we were in the line to buy tickets for the afternoon ferry to Athens. In the afternoon, we took the ferry – eight or nine hours, from Lesvos to Athens.

When we reached Athens harbour and left the ferry, we saw in front of us five or six buses, stopped, waiting for passengers. The drivers called, 'Hey, we are going to Macedonia, you can go with us.' We got in the bus immediately; we did not want to waste any time. We had heard that many people were ahead of us; nobody knew how long the borders would be open, so we were trying to pass through countries as quickly as possible. This part of the journey, I can't remember well. I was very tired!

We reached the Macedonia border; the buses stopped in a village, and we saw some Macedonian border soldiers. There were also some big tents. The soldiers directed us to them and told us, 'You should wait here until your time to cross.' It was very cold – there were no blankets, nothing. The tents were completely full, so we had to spend the night outside. At 7am, the soldiers formed us into two lines and two people at a time could cross the border. At 9.30am, we could successfully cross. The beauty of this journey was that we experienced many different kinds of transport! In some places we walked; in some places there were buses; in others, trains. I felt that I was, already, near to reaching my dream …

The Hungarian border had closed 20 days before this. So the soldiers there told us that 'You are in Croatia, and if you want to go to the next country – Slovenia – you have to get there by train. There is a very small train station, far from here. If you walk, it will take half a day. Or you can take a cab.' The soldiers pointed and told us, 'You can find private cars and taxis there – you should walk there.' We walked about one hour, and finally found lots of private cars waiting in a field. The police didn't allow them to come near the border. We talked with a driver, and took his car to the train station – about two hours. It was a very small, old station. It was raining – everywhere was wet, there was no food, no blankets, and it was 2am. The station was closed. Some local guys told us that 'everyday there is only one train from the station, exactly at 10am.' We went near to the old buildings, to protect us, and laid down. At 10.30am, the train came and all of the guys rushed to it. Some guys bought tickets; some, who hadn't enough money, didn't. I think the journey was six or eight hours to the Slovenian border; all the seats were full, we sat in the aisles.

At the border, the soldiers told us, 'You should wait, because we have a problem of lack of buses, until the buses come back.' We waited three hours. Then, more than ten buses arrived, and we got on, travelling towards the Austrian border. It was evening – 7 or 8pm With the help of the light from the buses, we could see that around the bus, it was like a jungle. After that, we crossed agricultural fields and went up and down some hills – another three hours. Slovenia was very beautiful.

We reached a place where there were three huge tents, with a capacity of maybe a thousand each. There were soldiers, who said they were Austrian border guards, who searched us quickly and directed us to the tents. We went inside, and they told us, 'You should wait, there are lots of people in front of you in the queue.' This was so familiar to us now: Wait, wait, queue, and queue. Midnight came. They gave us tuna fish, bread, coffee, tea, and told us to sleep on the camp beds – and wait. The tent was full of families. There were lots of facilities there for everything –portable toilets, places for washing and charging. We ate, some of us went to charge our cell phones. I and two other friends slept. It was the first time since we had entered Europe that we could relax.

The next day, at 4pm, was our time to cross. We walked for 3 or 4km beside the road until we reached another camp, with many tents and lots of people waiting in front of us. We waited a day there – 15 hours – for buses. When the buses came and we got on, we asked a soldier about the journey, and they said, 'You are going to a camp on the border of Austria and Germany.' The drivers said the same.

Three or four hours later, we reached the border; just before it, there were some small tents. The Austrian border soldiers told us to wait inside them, and one of them said, 'Do you see that river? That's the border. But first, you should wait!' I never asked the name of the river – I was just focused on getting across it.

It was night, 3.10am, when the soldiers told us, 'It's your turn: Go to the other side.' We crossed the bridge. On the other side we saw, like before, some tents, and immediately after the bridge, soldiers who told us, 'You are in Germany, welcome to our country!' They searched some of us, and very quickly – not our stuff; asked three or four questions about nationality, whether we were planning to stay, and whether we had fingerprints in any other country. Then they directed us to another tent, and said we should wait. After just twenty minutes, we got onto a bus. When we asked the soldier where we were going, he said, 'No one knows, but I think a place in the middle of the country, not near the border.'

Germany was the best organised of all. After roughly three hours' driving, we reached an old, unused factory with high walls. Inside there were camp beds, and they told us that, 'You should sleep here, and tomorrow we are going to transfer you to another camp.' We slept, and at 9am, another bus came and took us to a train station in this small town. There was a special train, just for refugees. The train left; as before, nobody knew our destination. This time, it took seven hours.

After the train stopped, buses transferred us to a huge camp with more than 20 buildings, in lines, with over 500 people in each one, partitioned – a previous military camp. It was really old. They told us, 'You should sleep, and tomorrow you should go to the administrative office, it's nearby, to get stuff like shampoo and soap, have a shower, and register for asylum, if you are staying.' They told us where the restaurant was – they showed us everything.

We were now just three friends. We lost the other two at a bus transfer. I stayed there just for three days. I left the camp by my own decision, with my friends, because we connected to some other friends who told us, 'If your situation is not so good, you can move to another city and camp.' During the three days, we talked with some other guys, and consulted with each other. And so we made a decision to go to another place – Cologne. So we left the camp for the train station and bought tickets for Cologne, at 11am.

I enjoyed Germany. During the five months, I travelled around to visit friends in many Germany cities. But when I compared it to the UK, the result was always that the UK was better for me. I had always planned to go to the UK, because of language and other things.

We always tracked news from our friends about the borders, using free wi-fi when we could. We got some news that it wasn't as bad as before – some friends had crossed to the UK. So during the five months, we had two different jobs. First, we were collecting news about friends who had successfully crossed to the UK, and the possibility that we could cross. Second, we were negotiating with some smugglers in Germany, to help us cross.

We found three smugglers, but we couldn't reach a successful deal with them. Some of our friends in Calais told us that 'The best way is to come here, because in this area you can find lots of smugglers, and there's no need to negotiate on the net or from Germany.'

In addition to banding together with other refugees, those who are on the move often gravitate towards familiar strangers – people who share a common ethnic or linguistic bond – for advice and guidance. However, there is little assurance that the guidance on offer is what is desired. Milkesa's new Ethiopian 'friends' in Europe betrayed him:

Milkesa (from Ethiopia):
I arrived in Italy's port, Catania on 25 June 2015. On the same day, the Italian government boarded me and other immigrants onto a minibus and we headed to Milan. We arrived in Milan on 26 June 2015. After about ten minutes of our arrival in Milan, where numerous immigrants from different countries camped, they transferred us into another minibus and then took us to Brescia's police division. The police told us to immediately leave Italy, saying Italy has no resources and capacity to resettle us, as the country is in an economic recession. The police further stated that the Italian population do not support further refugees' integration. Then after about a one-hour stay in this police division, they boarded us in the same minibus and took us to one of the churches in this

Brescia town, wherein they gave us lunch. After lunch they told us to leave, giving us our freedom to leave Italy. I would like to convey my heartfelt thanks and appreciation for the Italian government's humanitarian benevolence.

We left the church and scattered. I didn't know where to go. Every pedestrian I asked, from where I could board a train to Rome, spoke Italian and not English. Then I looked for people of black African descent like me, thinking that they could direct me. I came across many black persons but some of them spoke French while others spoke Italian. At that point, the only French word I knew was 'bonjour'. We went astray and were left with no hope. Finally we prayed for God to help us in our moment of difficulties.

Instead of rushing about together, I advised my Ethiopian friends from the boat to stay in a specific place, and I continued walking, together with one amongst my friends from my country who knew a little of the Somali language. We went to banks such as Western Union to try to change my US dollars into euros. All the banks I asked turned us away, saying that I couldn't change without a passport or any other valid identity document. Luckily, we came across a person of Somali origin who had Italian ID. This Somali man helped me with changing my money. Then I returned back to where I had left my friends and I asked if they want to change money. All of them except one told me that they didn't have any money for transportation fares. I promised to pay for all of them.

On the night of the 27th, we slept under trees in Brescia. Among us, there was a young guy; he came with me in the same boat from Egypt. He had a cousin and both were Ethiopian citizens of Somali origins. His cousin was an Italian citizen and she had lived in Naples for at least twenty years. The young guy made a telephone call to his cousin. He then told our group that his cousin wanted to accommodate us until she could arrange our safe journey to any destination among the European countries.

I bought a train ticket, even for this young guy. It cost €65 each from Brescia to Naples. So instead of going to Rome, I and the rest of my friends accompanied him to Naples. His cousin welcomed us at Naples train station. Then we walked for approximately eight minutes and she accommodated us in one of her Somalian brother's houses, which was about two or three minutes from her own house. In the course of our stay, I learned that this cousin and her Somali friend were smugglers and human traffickers. They made fraudulent passports at their house and sent immigrants to different European countries by land or by air.

This cousin and her Somali friend, whom we had thought were good Samaritans, held us for some days for ransom. She forced me to pay a great deal of money so that she could make a fake passport for me. She tried to convince me that it was impossible to cross to any other European country without a passport. But I instead told her to stop such fraudulent action and human trafficking. She threatened me. As I was already held as their captive, I gave her my friend's telephone number, who lives in Cairo as a political refugee under the UNHCR mandate. She cheated and convinced him to send 1,400 US dollars via a Somali money transfer. He sent it from Cairo to her. She then gave me €125 and told me to leave. I begged her to give me some more money of her own free will. She refused.

Among us, there was a man who had been an Oromo Liberation Front (OLF) member fighting against the Ethiopian government. This man was a 'dead alive' due to the inhuman torture that he had faced in Ethiopian prisons. He didn't know even a word of the English language. I humbly beseeched the woman for this old man to accompany me. 'He can't go without paying,' she said. No captives could leave without her consent. I worried for the old man and I started recording everything in my memory to confide to the police station nearest to her house. I abstained myself from actually reporting, just turning and tossing many things in my memory. This old man had no source of money. I decided not to step outdoors and leave the old man behind. I decided to face whatever fate would come in my life: to die and save him, or to die before he would die.

But then the young man, this woman's cousin, warned he would kill me with the cooperation of her friends. Later, this man tried to take revenge against the rest of my friends one by one. Each captive was waiting in suspense until their turn would arrive to be released after somebody had intervened with money. The young man later asked for asylum in Austria.

The lack of security experienced in earlier stages of the journey is therefore not limited to the countries where the authors first sought refuge. It is also reproduced on arrival to the first port of call in Europe, prompting a need to keep on moving.

Eritrea (from Eritrea):
In Sicily, they kept us in a wide building for five days. After five days, we started shouting. People forget the challenges that they have been through, all they remember is their ambition: where should they go? That was their way of thinking. Actually, the situation made us shout because most of the people needed to have care for their health. The Italians asked us what was happening and we told them, 'We want to move on from here, so why are you keeping us?' They told us, 'You can leave tomorrow, don't worry.' They took us by bus to different parts of Italy.

They took me to Venice but they did not give me a room. I did not have any other option than to continue to Milan where I stayed for two days. There I got food from charities, but there were no places to stay. A smuggler asked where I was from – I didn't know his name but he was from Eritrea. We asked him where we should go and he told us that Italy is not a good place to stay. 'It is bullshit', he said. It would be better to go to the UK, he told me, because I am educated, because I speak English and because I am able to communicate with the people there. 'UK has a good asylum support', he told me. I asked him, 'But don't other countries have good asylum support?' 'I don't know, but UK is better', he said. I asked him how I could get to the UK. He said he could take me there himself, so we went to a train station. He asked us to

VOICES FROM THE JUNGLE

pay him but we had no money. He told us to call our
relatives and then they could pay him. We didn't have
an option: our relatives should pay the money in order
for us to reach our destination.

We got on a train to Ventimiglia, and from there we
got a car. There is a chain there between the smugglers.
We went by car to Nice, by bus from Nice to Antibes,
train from Antibes to Paris and from there we went by
train to Calais. That was the journey until Calais. I did
not expect to face further challenges there.

Eritrea's story of his journey through Europe is relatively
short; Milkesa's, taking in being held hostage, much longer.
Travelling in family groups also lengthened the trip. Safia
and her husband had to make the journey with three small
children:

Safia (from Afghanistan):
It has been 11 months now since I left Afghanistan.
We came by airline to Iran, then we walked to Turkey
and after Turkey we took a boat, a little boat, then on
foot. Then Macedonia, Serbia. It was dangerous with
the children. They had a life jacket but it was not so
good with the three children. It took three months to
come. We were in Germany before arriving in Calais
and we arrived in April 2016.

The problems of travelling within Europe were, for Refugees'
Voice, of a more general kind. Desperate for status, and
advised by trusted friends that he could get papers quickly
in Italy, he found, like Milkesa, that Italy was keen for
refugees to leave and not able to support them:

Refugees' Voice (from Afghanistan):
Then I realised that three to five million people are jobless in Italy. So I thought if I am asking for asylum here, what am I going to do here afterwards? I spent two days in Italy, then two days in France; then I went to Belgium, and then came back to France again, to Calais.

Mapping fear and desire

Phases of the journey hold particular anxieties and fears. For Shaheen, these were to be found first in the treacherous crossings of the Aegean Sea and then later in the foreboding forests of Eastern Europe:

Shaheen (from Afghanistan):
So the day came. They took us to the beach – that was around midnight. Then they pumped the boat. The boat was just for five people and they put 22 of us in it. There was a small engine on the boat. They started the engine, and we sat in the boat. Then they showed us a light glimmering in the distance. They said, 'That is Greece, and you have to go towards that light'; and we started our journey.

After two hours and even with the best of luck, we found ourselves at the midway point and out of fuel. There was 20 litres of petrol with us at the start that the agents had given us, and we put in the petrol; that was at around three o'clock. The sea waves were very powerful and scary. There were two women and three children with us; they were crying. So we started the boat engine again. We moved towards the small flickering light.

We had been travelling for an hour after we re-started, when we realised we had lost our way. Someone was saying we should go to the right, and another was saying to the left.

Then, unfortunately, the air from the boat began seeping out. Someone shouted, 'Hey, the boat is going soft!' Right away, I knew that there was a hole in the boat. Everybody started checking their life jackets.

With a sudden powerful wave of water, we were submerged under. In a minute, we lost each other. The water was cold and my jaws started shaking; I couldn't even shout and water had gone in my mouth; I started choking. The water was extremely salty. After about twenty minutes, I saw some people in life jackets, so I shouted out at them.

That was a very hard time for me. There are no words with me to explain that situation. May Allah save everyone from that situation. Finally, I was thinking that these were the last moments of my life. I said, crying, 'I can't save my life; now I am dying, Please God help me for my children, help me for my good deeds and good dealings with people.' I even lost my voice.

After an hour, I saw a light in the distance. I thought my head was spinning, but really the light was coming toward me, and thanks be to God, it was a Turkish police boat. I just raised my hands and they shouted in a loudspeaker. Again, I raised my hands and they saw me, and they took me. It was only when they put me in the boat with them that I closed my eyes.

I saw when I opened my eyes after two or three hours that there were only five of us. I was surprised that we were a group of 22 but now only five. I asked the policeman, 'Where are the others?' He said, 'We just found you five boys.' I shouted, 'We were 22 persons!' Then they started searching again, but unfortunately they didn't find anyone else. I cried so much, and then I asked them about one of my friends by the name of Haroon. The officer asked the boys on the other side, 'Anyone by the name of Haroon here?' Haroon shouted, 'I am Haroon!' I heard the voice, and then I became happy, a little bit. 'Thanks to Allah, one of my friends is saved.' Then the police took us to the hospital, because some of us were a little bit sick. They treated us well, and two days later, they left us in Istanbul.

Shaheen's story is long, with many false starts and dead ends. Another frightening episode occurred in Bulgaria:

Eventually, we reached a deep dark jungle; it was about nine o'clock at night. The agents told us, 'We have to sleep here for some hours and also take some food.' We were very tired, so all the boys slept. Suddenly, at around 11 o'clock, a boy shouted, and everyone woke up. It was extremely dark; I don't really know how to explain what happened next. We all started shouting. The agent said, 'Stay together, don't move!' Suddenly, we saw red eyes like lights just surrounding us. The agent shouted, 'They are ghosts, they want to harm us – just recite some verses of the Quran!' When we all started reciting the Quran, with some us crying, 'O, Allah save us from these things!' They stopped coming towards us.

So after some minutes these things left us, they disappeared, but from far away, the ghosts were still crying out and making some horrible sounds. I can't explain it; it was incredibly horrible. All night long we stayed awake; we were just trembling – our whole bodies were shaking.

Once in Europe, the decision to keep moving depends on whether expectations regarding security are met on arrival. Here is Mohammed Ahmed once more:

Mohammed Ahmed (from Sudan):
When we reached Italy, we spent some days in a refugee camp, but the camp was boring and there was not enough food, and the place was so cold. Then we decided to cross to France, because people told us to leave Italy, because there is nothing there at all. We found some other people who were also going to France; then we crossed to France and went to the Calais camp which was full of refugees. We met some friends in the camp but we found the same things: there is not enough food, and the weather was so cool, and there were no houses in which to stay, and no covers, and no clothes to wear. We suffered a lot, and until now we are still suffering in the Calais camp.

For others, safety was never envisioned to be in Europe. The physical challenges and difficulties met on the journey means people want to keep on moving.

Africa (from Sudan):

It was never my plan or my dream to come to Europe. I would have been happy even to stay in Egypt. Any place to make me safe, that was all I wanted. It was not my choice to come here, I came here by force. I do not like Europe, I am sorry to say that, because it is not my culture, and even it is not my language. I didn't know them, they didn't know me. Because of that I didn't want to choose Europe. Never. Never. Even on the religious side. I am a Muslim. I know there are Muslims in Europe and that they are free to pray or not to pray. I know that. But what about my mother? How could I look after her? If I was there in Egypt I can work; I know myself; I can work everywhere. But how about safety? You couldn't find it anywhere else. When I moved to Europe, I decided to stay in Italy; ok it's safe, it's good. But when I asked, a lot of people were there two, three years, in the camp, with no papers. It is not life. I came to Paris and went to La Chapelle Metro, I went to the Jean-Quarre school camp; I saw people living under a bridge. This is not a safe life. This is not the life I am looking for.

I heard about Germany, I heard about many, many countries. Someone told me if you go to Calais maybe you can reach the UK. It is like an adventure, do you know, like when you are a kid looking for adventures? I am like an island, swimming, take me anywhere, anywhere. Okay, let me go to there.

There is no singular refugee experience or journey. While there are common tropes to be found in many accounts – the evasion of authority figures, dealings with unscrupulous

smugglers, and camaraderie with other fellow migrants –
how that journey unfolded is retold to give sense to the
odyssey. Majid, whose journey featured prominently earlier
in this chapter was keen to emphasise time and time again
his own decision-making in undertaking the journey – how
he is 'someone who loves new and difficult things,' adding
'for me, this journey was exciting – a big adventure.' On
navigating the Aegean, he tells us: 'It was exciting for me – I
love challenges. Instead of being afraid, I was so happy to be
leaving my country, because I love freedom.'

We conclude this chapter by returning to Muhammad's
account of his journey in which he sketches a map of desire
onto the journey.

Muhammad (from Syria):
How can we start? From the day I left Diyarbakir,
with friends' tears and heartbreaks that say these moments will never come back again, the plan was to
make a journey for life; to leave alone, with nothing
but the mercy of God; to try to live in poverty and
hopeless conditions, of hunger and fear, faithless; with
the real difficulties of trying to protect the people you
love; feeling the reality of deprivation, injustice and
weakness. It was about a new experience of life.

And for me, I would start a special journey for my
life goals and to expand my knowledge. (I didn't tell
anyone else about this plan.) I was in Izmir for two days:
in the hands of smugglers, with my family, people who
trust just in you. It was my first time dealing with such
issues, but I was able to succeed in this test, encouraged
by my sister. I think we could, together, teach some
smugglers how to be careful and respect people.

Our 'realtor' – the agent working between us and the smugglers – was from Kobanî himself. He was a very bad person. He bought us very bad diving vests and air rubber donuts, although we had paid a heavy price for them. He tried to trade our lives. We discovered it after we rode the sea. Luckily, we didn't need them.

We arrived in Greece, on the island of Chios, at 4.30am, and because we got wet, my mobile phone was damaged, and it was cold. The second day, I sent my group, as I had planned, before me, on the ship from Chios to Kavala in Greece. I had to find an excuse not to go with them; they discovered I was not with them when they were on the ship. I was watching their progress step by step, to make sure that they would arrive safely – that was my promise to my brother. When I was assured that they were safe, I started my journey.

I had decided that I should make it an interesting journey, in order to feel like a refugee, using the hardest way and method. I wanted to feel the real life of the refugees, and to try to travel without feeling that there is someone who can support me.

After walking more than 30km and sleeping outside in the cold, I went to a camp on Chios. I had lost most of my money, so I had to be careful. I slept four days in the camp, in the December cold. Every day, I had only one potato sandwich at night to eat, to save what little money I had (I still had a little in another pocket because I usually separate the money in many places). There were Greek organisations which brought food sometimes, but that time I decided not to eat in the camp, and I was fasting for two days.

FIGURE 2.2
In Greece. Photo by Muḥammad (from Syria).

I met some guys, three from Kurdistan and one from Syria. We started a journey together from that island to Kavala and from there to Macedonia. It took several days. It was snowing that first night. We left Macedonia for Serbia by train, and then by walking. It was a really frozen day. When we travelled from Macedonia to Serbia, we had to walk for a distance between the two borders. On that road, there were many Serbian smugglers who were trying to rob people. There were taxi drivers who were telling people, 'The train station is too far, we will take you but only for €100, or €50, or €20' (it depended on the passenger). Some people went with them. And some people were taken to a different place and robbed. But for us, we

FIGURE 2.3
Serbian train. Photo by Muhammad (from Syria).

discovered that there is an organisation on the other side, in Serbia; they gave food and hot drinks and even free transportation by buses. All these volunteers were German, so I guess that it was a German organisation.

We then left Serbia by a train, and it was the worst train in the world. People were like sheep: no place for most of us to sit, even between the seats. You could find children under the seats sleeping. It was very cold, and very slow. We arrived in Croatia, where they checked me, and from there went to Slovenia, where they checked me again, but this time they took all of my medical things and cigarette lighters. I always have lighters and a small knife with me for fire and food. (I hate smoking. And I even don't drink tea or coffee. Only juice and water and sometimes cola.)

We arrived in Austria, and from there went to Germany where the German Army and the Red Cross took us to Munich. For the first time since I left Izmir, I could have a shower, but I got ill after that. My suitcase was about 35–40kg. I was holding it on my back, and lacked sleep. Over the course of six days, I don't remember that I had slept more than six or seven hours. But I am accustomed to hard conditions. I used to work in a war zone 'hospital'; I'm a doctor, so it is not strange for me to stay awake for more than thirty hours, and sometimes more than two days. But when I sleep I can sleep for a very long time. (It is like recharging). I was then in a very bad situation, with fever and difficulty in breathing, sweating, anorexia and really muddled in my mind.

In fact, it was a wonderful journey for me: I'm happy I took it. The journey inside Germany is another story.

CHAPTER 3

Living in the 'Jungle':
Arriving, exploring and settling in

Africa (from Sudan):
Go anywhere in the Jungle, say, 'Hi',
and you will hear, 'Hi, please come on in'.
Because of that, I find this place wonderful.

Milkesa (from Ethiopia):
My time in the 'Jungle' –
it was from insanity to death.

Introduction

After long and hazardous journeys, all the authors of this book arrived at the 'Jungle' refugee camp outside Calais in northern France. In this chapter, authors present their accounts of their early time in the 'Jungle': a place no one wants to live in, yet also a place that camp residents made into a valued temporary home.

We begin with Muhammad's description of how he arrived. This frightening and bewildering time also contained the seeds of his later more positive experiences in the camp.

Muhammad arrived in Calais aiming, like most in the camp, to travel to the UK. He did not, like many others, have a legal right to UK asylum through having family in the UK, or a history of working with UK forces, or through his own vulnerability;[1] but he had other strong reasons:

Muhammad (from Syria):
Many things make people try to go to the UK. Some of them have families or relationships in UK. Others want to go because of the language; I love the English language. And some people want to go because England has a small number of refugees, so they think the situation will be better for them. I don't know exactly what was the reason for me. I dreamed of a chance to take a PhD in a famous university. I thought that it would be better to have science education from these places; they could improve my skills more than others. Most surgical research references are in English. I heard that England is a place where the law and freedom have more respect than other countries. I have many British friends on the Internet; I really wanted to see them. And more than that, I was excited about having a journey to discover life in the hardest way possible. These motivations are complicated; you can't focus on anything on its own.

I started to think seriously about going to the UK as soon as I arrived in Germany. I was excited about travelling to England. But by chance, I chose the most difficult and cold time to go. The plan was that I would try for about 15 to 20 days. If I succeeded, I would be in London. If not, I would go back and in addition I

1 Regulation (EU) No 604/2013 of the European Parliament and of the Council of 26 June 2013: http://eur-lex.europa.eu/legal-content/EN/TXT/PDF/?uri=CELEX:32013R0604&from=EN (accessed 21 October 2016).

would have improved my skills and experience about life. So I had a clear goal and purpose.

After one day trying to sneak onto the Eurostar train in Paris, which seemed impossible to me, and walking in the streets and stations, I reached Calais at night. Although I had a map, I didn't know the way, and I was afraid of the police. From 5pm to 7pm, I was looking for the camp; I passed through so many areas. Finally, I followed some guys who looked to be from the camp (they were Afghans) and arrived there. Later, friends told me that the way I took was the most dangerous road, because it is controlled by smugglers who hit anyone who attempts to take that way, to preserve that route to the car ferry for themselves.

Anyway, when I arrived at the camp, I was surprised that I saw no houses, no electricity; there were just shelters, and some tents and strange people (so many strange and scary faces). I arrived after two days of travelling with an empty stomach and a broken foot (no one hit me – my foot broke for another reason, but I didn't realise that at first. It is a long story!), knowing no one, with no connections, to see a place that belonged to the European Middle Ages.

My spirits fell to below zero. I tried to look for some Syrian Kurds, but I failed to find any. I came on a small, deserted tent. It was dirty and filled with rubbish. I cleaned it a little, and lay on the ground for an hour. I was so tired, but I couldn't sleep. I was afraid of robbers, it was very cold, and my foot was hurting me. So I left that tent and started walking in the camp, looking for someone. At that time, I realised that there is always one thing harder than whatever you have seen. And this was the worst thing I had seen until now. But maybe there is something worse than that worst thing, too. Sometimes when you feel that things are getting bad, you expect that it could be worse. I was thinking like that: 'It is very bad now, but I think it will be very very very bad later.'

Eventually, I saw people speaking Arabic; they seemed to be from Syria, so I asked them some questions: 'Where can I buy a sim card for the Internet, where can I find some people from Kobanî?', etc. They were kind people; they invited me to their tent to have dinner, and guided me to a tent of Kobanîs, but it was empty. Those people were out, trying to sneak onto the lorries near the train station, and they didn't come back that night.

The next morning, I went to see those guys from Kobanî. They were still sleeping. The first man I saw who was awake, had strange features on his face, with a thick beard, but he looked friendly inside – that was my feeling. His name was Ahmed and this man would become one of my best friends. He started to say 'Welcome' as soon as I entered the cold, white tent. And then he said, 'I think that I know you, aren't you Dr Muhammad?' I was the leader of a medical department in Kobanî for more than two years, and I trained many staff and volunteers on basic medical nursing and first aid. Ahmed was working in the hospital as a volunteer at that time. The second man I met was Mustafa, a very kind person. Anyway, soon, all of them woke up. They were four boys from Kobanî, and one from Al-Qamishli.

Later, I went with Mustafa and Ahmed to see the different places in the camp, and the organisations. They took me to a place where Syrian Kurds lived. Again, when first I saw them, they looked strange and scary, but soon, all these feelings would change. They took me to the main Syrian Kurdish shelter, with the Kurdish flag fluttering above it. I saw three other people there – Faisal, Fouad, Anur – who would later become part of my family in Calais.

Muhammad's story sets the scene for the exhausting work of surviving in the 'Jungle', spending your nights attempting physically demanding and dangerous breaches of near-impenetrable security barriers, yet still finding helpfulness, friendship, even a kind of family, in the camp.

The rest of this chapter presents authors' stories of the hardship, weariness, insecurity and depression that engulfed people when they started to live in the camp, before moving on to stories of what they have learned and the communities that they found and made in their early days there.

Rejecting the 'Jungle': 'We are not animals'

Unlike Muhammad, some authors of this book decided to write very little about the 'Jungle' itself. Milkesa, for instance, wrote just the single, vivid line at the very beginning of this chapter. Other authors, however, spent a great deal of time using photographs, commentary on them, and other writing, to denounce living conditions in the 'Jungle'.

FIGURE 3.1

All over, it's full of water, it's like a river here. Nobody can pass,
because it's too muddy. Photo by Habibi (from Afghanistan).

Living like animals

Habibi had, as he recounted in Chapter 1, escaped the
Taliban to travel across Europe. He took many photographs
of the poor conditions of the 'Jungle' and commented on
the shame of such ways of living:

> *Habibi (from Afghanistan):*
> My parents are in Afghanistan. I didn't tell them, 'I'm
> living in the "Jungle".' When my mum calls, I say,
> 'Actually yeah, they gave me a very nice house here.'
> Sometimes they tell me, 'Send me a picture.' I go to a
> volunteer's house, taking pictures of it, sending them
> to them. As if I have a really nice house. I cannot tell
> them the truth, that I'm living the 'Jungle' life. And the

tent: for four-and-a-half months I was living in a tent.
But now I've got a shelter, for two days up till now.

Babak, recently arrived from Iran, pointed out the problems
of fires in tents, though not in the few French govern-
ment-constructed containers which housed 1,500 people
after the south zone of the camp was demolished in March
2016. Babak moved into the containers as soon as they
became available:

Babak (from Iran):
When I lived in a tent, it was in the winter and we
made a fire inside to get warm. When we put out the
fire, it was very cold, it was like a freezer. When I woke
up at 8am in the morning I escaped the tent because
it was so cold, I couldn't stay inside. It was warmer
outside. The water on top of the tent was like ice in
a freezer. Every day it is cold outside, so people make
a fire. I understand why people do this, but it is dangerous because of the smoke you breathe in. I think it
is better to stay in the container. It is a small container
for twelve people, but I think it is better than the tent.

Teddy described a recent facility in the camp, built after
the March 2016 evictions but nevertheless not adequate for
habitation:

Teddy (from Eritrea):
The blue tents were erected by the government after
the demolition. There are up to 15 people in a tent; it
is very crowded.

FIGURE 3.2

This picture shows the situation of migrants: how to live, how to cook. This is a new area. My house is behind the tent. There is a water vessel in the foreground. The tie in the front of the picture is securing the tent. It is cemented in. Photo by Teddy (from Eritrea).

When the weather is cold, people warm themselves by burning some wood – and also plastic, because we don't get enough wood. There could be so many consequences, such as respiratory disease. These plastics are hazardous, affecting the lungs and causing environmental pollution, like climate change. This is because the people are not aware about these things.

Zeeshan Javid, also living in one of the containers, described the shame of them, again starting from one of his pictures:

FIGURE 3.3
Containers. Photo by Zeeshan Javid (from Pakistan).

Zeeshan Javid (from Pakistan):
If I show a photo of the container where I live to my mother, she will ask me to come back because she doesn't know. They think I live in this house and that I have this car. When we call home we say we are in Paris. We don't say we are in Calais. It is because we don't want to make our parents sad. If they tell us to come back home, and if we go back home, then we must go and fight.

One of the women living in the camp, Safia, from Afghanistan, also described the difficulties of camp life, including the specific problems that arose for the women living there with young children and with their husbands:

Safia (from Afghanistan):
When we arrived I said to my children, 'It is so dirty', and I told them we were not going to stay for a long time, that we are going to the UK. When I had the baby and I went to the Jules Ferry Centre[2], I got a big room and many women came together to live. But still I prefer to live in a caravan because there are not too many people. In the Jules Ferry Centre, there will be 14 or 16 women all together in one room with the children. I chose the caravan for the little one, so the baby can be quiet, and I can be with my husband, which is not possible in the Jules Ferry Centre – he has to live outside it. You need your husband close to you to help you. It would be harder to be without my husband.

The containers are not so good because there is no good behaviour. But the container was for six persons and I have a newborn so it would have been better; now we have only one caravan for the six of us. It is not decent, there are big holes and it is windy. Here it is mainly Kurdish families. All the women around are Kurdish and Afghani in the caravans. So we connect with the people in this area.

They gave us one caravan. But there are no toilets. We don't have anything, no washing machine for washing the clothes, and everything is dirty, there are lots of bacteria. I can take a shower in the caravan, sometimes. There is a shower there. This is the only place I can go; and sometimes, at the Salam Centre – but I can't go because I am not registered at Salam so I don't have access. So the women

2 The French government-run Jules Ferry Centre provided accommodation for some women and children, and showers and meals for other camp residents.

in the camp, they can't have a shower in Salam, you need to register. If you don't register at Salam, you can't. If you register, then you have to go with your children. One day, I went alone to take a shower and they said no.

When I was pregnant, I went to see sometimes the midwives at Salam. But here it is not good for the babies. They haven't got immunisation such as for tuberculosis. Maybe there is tuberculosis in the camp because of the bacteria. I wanted the baby to have the vaccine but one week I went; then they said, 'You need to come the day after.' Then I went and she said, 'Come back again.' After three days, she said there weren't any vaccines left. I am worried for the baby, the caravan is not good for him. My other children are immunised, they had their vaccine in Afghanistan.

To have the little baby, I went with an ambulance to the hospital and I stayed there three days and then I came back. My husband was there with me when I gave birth. The children were being looked after by the volunteers. During the day, they were going to the blue bus, the Unofficial Women's and Children's Centre, and my husband was with me. He came back for the night to look after them. I also saw a paediatrician in Calais afterwards but the baby hasn't got any vaccinations yet.

Humanity denied

We have heard from Safia that the relatively safe spaces available for women and children run by the French government just outside the camp disconnected them from husbands and fathers. Within the camp itself, beyond physical problems, the 'Jungle' was, authors often said, a cause of shame and loss of human connection.

Mani wrote several poems about the despair attached to the camp, even its apparently positive aspects like fires; feelings of exclusion from places of worship, and the loss of mothers, as well as writing about an image of a mother that he stencilled all over the camp for Mothers' Day:

Mani (from Iran)
Every night,
Around the fire,
I don't know –
We burned our wood
Or hopes.
When I went to the church they told me, 'You are a Muslim',
When I went to the mosque they told me, 'You are Christian.'
I prefer to come back to my shelter to pray to god.

My mother: You are so far, so far. What can I say? Just, 'I miss you', not more, not less.

For more than 15 years, every mother's day
I bought a present for my mother.
This year I was in the 'Jungle'; I didn't have any money for buying anything and if I had money we couldn't post anything.
Suddenly I thought,
'Here there are a lot of journalists.

FIGURE 3.4
My mother: You are so far, so far. What can I say?
Just, 'I miss you', not more, not less. Stencil by Mani (from Iran).

If I do
Something interesting for them,
Maybe she will see it in Iran and will be happy.'

Containers also do not address the issue of dehumanisation. Babak, like several authors, had claimed asylum in France; some, like Milkesa, were dispersed and housed. Those whose claims were first refused, like Babak, had nowhere to stay. He was living wherever he could for free: first in a tent and then a shipping container while he appealed against the decision. His status meant he was erased as a person in other ways:

Babak (from Iran):

I arrived on the 4th December 2015. I am from Iran. I tried to get to the UK and that was when I got arrested. I spent one month in detention. I asked for asylum in France during detention, and I have papers that show I have asked for asylum. I asked for refugee status in France, because the first country in which I felt safe was here. It was good for me.

But very fast, they did an interview with me. They brought me to the OFPRA[3] office and they rejected me very fast. And after that, I went to some refugee association and there I asked for a lawyer and they told me, 'You can have a lawyer and then you can make an appeal against the decision.' I must wait maybe six months or nine months. They said, 'Because you were rejected first, you won't have any place to stay from the French government.' So I have no choice, I am just still here to wait for the next chance. I have nowhere to live. So I must stay here.

When you ask for asylum at the asylum office in France, they give you a photo and identity paper that says when you asked for asylum. When you ask for asylum in the detention centre, they just give you a paper without any photo, so you can't even go to the hospital with that. It just says that you were in detention and asked for asylum.

When I am talking with my mum and explain I am in a container, she says, 'Why a container? Is it small?' I say, 'No.' I try to go somewhere else to have good-quality reception, and then I explain good things to

---

3 OFPRA: *Office française de protection des réfugiés et apatrides.* The French Office for the Protection of Refugees and Stateless Persons.

her. I tell her that I am good. I don't want to show my family what is happening here. I always tell that I am good and that I am living in a house. My mother doesn't have Facebook, so most things my family don't know.

She knows that I am in the camp but I told her now that I am not living in the camp. I just say that I come here to do some work, do photography and work for a friend. I don't explain to her that I am living here. Before, I told her, but she got really upset. She told me to leave and go to my uncle's house. He is living in Malmö in Sweden. I told her that I am here and that they gave me an apartment and that I am doing really good. I sent her pictures of my friend's house so she thinks I live there. I told her a lie because I don't want her to worry.

After a rainy night, sunlight through the room's window wakes me up. I take a look at my mobile's watch and I also look around. I see 11 persons, 11 room mates, 11 fellow travellers; we're so close to each other and so far from each other at the same time. We're so close because all of us sleep in the small container, and we are so far because each one of us has a different point of view about his future. I go outside in order to avoid the container's narrow space, I walk in mud caused by last night's rain, and loaf around with my ideas. I occasionally ask myself, 'What would happen?', sunk in my good and bad scenarios about my future. I gaze at other people's eyes.

Today is Saturday and so many volunteers have come for a visit. They look at me, and they are shocked. As we get closer, I try to say hello in their language, and I smile, and they give a smile and they say hello, and they look at me differently from how they did before. Seemingly, they were waiting for a weird event to happen, but they finally saw a human that has a different skin colour and different hair colour and has a different culture and language since he's come from a long way away. I sink in my ideas again. This time, I think, 'What's the difference between us? Maybe it's because they do not know me; maybe we met in an inappropriate place; maybe if they had seen me in a coffee shop or in a bus station in another city, they would have another idea about me; maybe they made a bad prejudgement.' A judgement derived from the media, which all show their own preferred images to feed their needs.

But the truth is not what they say. A migrant is not only a word, not only news, not only a problem for society: a human is living behind this word. He has feelings, hope for future, and there are some people waiting for him to come back, and a family waiting for good news. The problem is that they've only shown the bad points of the 'Jungle', while there exist good points and bad points in all societies. Also, in this 'Jungle', in the hardest situation, good things still exist. There are people here who want to live in a free society, they want to be educated, work, learn, experience and develop and live independent of any religion. There are people who have passed through the hardest and the most dangerous way to reach their hopes. Maybe these people are around you. It's true that they've come to your city and made some problems but these people can live a life like yours in the future, in your society. They are people who need attention and education.

*

I have a shopping list, is there someone going to the city centre?

I want to cook a soup for the 'Jungle'.

Please buy a little smile I want for the surly face of the police.

Please buy a little chance for my unlucky friends that want to go to England.

Please buy a little manhood for acquisitive smugglers.

Please buy a little solidarity for all nationalities here.

Please buy responsibility for the respectable English government!

Please buy a little courage I want for the quiet lips of refugees.

Please buy a little game for little children in the camp.

Please buy an empty mind, this one I want for myself.

FIGURE 3.5
Cooking in the 'Jungle'. Photo by Babak (from Iran).

The 'Jungle' 'inside

As these stories tell us, the difficulties of the 'Jungle' were not just physical, but psychological, social and philosophical. Ali, who arrived in Calais with Babak, gave this account of these difficulties and how people – including himself – addressed them:

Ali (from Iran):
I think, myself, that this is a bad situation, with bad problems, but very different people are here. Because they can't find out what the problem is, they think, 'If we go to England, we can earn powerful money and we can come back to our country. We can live with that money.' But they have the problem inside themselves; they can't find the problem.

It's morning! Is it morning? No, it's midday. I open my eyes, I wish I could sleep more because time is better when asleep.

The bitter feeling of the morning will come out with repeated coughs. It seems like it's Sunday.

The 'Jungle' on a Sunday.

It's full of volunteers. Full of kind hello with pity. Pity!

Sundays in the 'Jungle': pity. Outside of the 'Jungle': hatred.

I can't find peace except by fighting against these reactions. Because I don't understand their language?

But the problem is not the language. The problem is the prison that I have built for myself. I don't even understand the Iranian language anymore.

Everything I knew before I got here has changed

FIGURE 3.6
This is a bad situation, with bad problems.
Photo by Ali (from Iran).

since I first arrived! Because here, in such a small place, there are thousands of people more than ten nationalities, a hundred cultures and thousands of different ideas and beliefs.

It is because of this that I say that I can't find my peace; I can't find my peace except for fighting with these reactions. The purpose of my fight isn't exactly the thing that you are thinking about now!

And maybe it's my problem that we can't understand each other's languages.

Living with violence

Authors wrote of the hostility and violence both inside and outside the camp, that also denied refugees' humanity. These events affected everyone: those trying to claim asylum in France, as well as those trying to get to the UK:

> *Zeeshan Imayat (from Pakistan):*
> When you are a poor man, no one is your friend. When you are rich, everyone is your friend. Everyone tells you. 'Welcome.' When you have good shoes, good pants, a good shirt, good clothes, everyone will tell you, 'Hello', 'Hi', 'Come here.' When you have no good shoes, good clothes, no one will notice you. Everyone respects you just for your clothes and your shoes, not for your heart – they don't see your heart. They see just what you look like. Sometimes French people, when you go to Calais city, they will ignore you. Why? We are all human. That is a mistake and it happens because we are refugees.

Violence was most immediately experienced from police – especially the French riot police, the *Compagnies Républicaines de Sécurité*, or CRS – charged with stopping camp residents getting to the UK. It affected even those claiming or planning to claim asylum in France, such as Babak and Ali, or Zeeshan Javid, who because of prior fingerprinting as we heard in the previous chapter could not claim asylum for several months. He contrasted this ongoing aggression with his previous and wished-for future life:

> *Zeeshan Javid (from Pakistan):*
> The UK pay the French government so they will beat the people or spray with gas. We hate the police, and we hate the journalists. They just write your story

FIGURE 3.7
Some camp residents' views of the police.
Photo by Zeeshan Javid (from Pakistan).

and then they go back. They don't help you or anything. Now we need help. We have talent and we need
freedom. If they would just give me the documents!
I have talent and I was studying in Pakistan. If they
would just give me college or university! We have
talent and we are young boys. They didn't give me any
chance. We are 19 and 20 years old. When we sit with
friends in the camp restaurants , we are talking about
what we can do.

This morning we went to the office and they told us
that we have to wait for four more months. We arrived
together from Pakistan in July 2015. We are cousins.
First, we tried to get to the UK, but one of our cousins
died in a train accident here, trying to get to the UK.
We want to apply for asylum here in France; we will
do it later this year because we have to wait for six

months because we were fingerprinted in Bulgaria.[4] In the 'Jungle', we have the problem that we don't have any facilities. We have many problems. No organisation will give us help.

Haris, also from Pakistan, wrote about camp violence, too, starting from his images:

Haris (from Pakistan):
In some of the pictures I took, I put myself in a very dangerous position. When the police saw a camera in my hand, he pointed at me and said, 'Don't come here or I will shoot you'; he had a tear-gas gun in his hand. That was one week ago. Normally the police don't do that, but sometimes there is a traffic jam on the motorway so people want to go and try to get to the UK. The police try to stop people.

They use tear gas and throw water from the water truck to stop the people. They use that a lot. I can see it from where my tent is. This is people running from tear gas.

Babak described the surveillance mechanisms around the edge of the camp, which operated to alert the police, and functioned as another kind of fence:

---

4 The Dublin III Treaty says refugees must claim asylum in the first European country they reach. A European country can refuse a refugee's asylum claim if there is fingerprint or other evidence that they spent time in another European country, and they can be deported to that European country. However, many European countries now have an additional qualification that allows appeal, after an initial claim refusal, if the refusal was made on the grounds of fingerprinting in some other countries. This qualification applies in France. See the Welcome to Europe site: http://w2eu.info/.

FIGURE 3.8

They use tear gas and they throw water from the water truck to stop the people. They use that a lot. I can see it from where my tent is. This is people running from tear gas. Photo by Haris (from Pakistan).

Babak (from Iran):
There is a road outside the camp. It is the road the refugees walk, when they go and try to get to the UK. The road the refugees take to try to get to the UK is a bad and dangerous passage. It is covered with lights. I felt really bad when I saw this defence to protect the way and also to floodlight. It is like going from the dark into the light.

Shikeb, working as a volunteer in one of the camp schools, had seen many instances of both police and personal violence:

Shikeb (from Afghanistan):

I could show you many people here who have put cigarettes out on their arms.

And now I am going to tell an amazing thing. There was an Iranian here, his wife was pregnant.

The French said, 'If you don't put your fingerprints, we'll give your baby to another family.' He did, and the government promised, 'We'll give you a house and €1,000 a month.'

After he did the fingerprints, they said, 'You go back to the "Jungle".' He went back and checked, and the government did not give the money. And now, the mother's milk is not coming …

Some time ago, I was injured – someone hit me. The person who attacked me said, 'Why did I do this? I am sorry.' Recently, his brother came looking for him; I went to where he had been living to try to find him, and they told me he was now sick and in the hospital. People here have problems – often they are sad for a long time.

Perhaps the most thoroughgoing critical account of the camp was given by Africa, whose route, as we heard in the previous chapter, took him from Sudan, through Libya and Egypt to the hoped-for safety of Europe:

Africa (from Sudan):

It was big trouble for me when I came to Calais. I couldn't believe that this is Europe. Is it true that this place exists in Europe? Where is humanity, where is democracy? Where is all this bullshit? They just write it in the paper. I think, because we have come here, we are not human beings, we become animals, a new kind of animal. A new kind of animal that has developed at this time; it's known as 'refugee'.

We came here to see this really 'dignified' European life. Yes, I like it; it is a good life for the people. I don't want to talk about differences between white people and black people. It is like we have been deserted. Because this is Europe, a place of humanity.

Many people ask me why I haven't applied for asylum in France. But this situation, here in the 'Jungle', is not likely to be one that encourages anyone to get registered in France.

Thinking outside the 'Jungle'

Such negative assessments of the camp were, for some authors, almost beside the point, because of their other concerns. As he described in Chapter 1, Teza had had to leave Iran suddenly, with his wife, who was now in the UK. He now had a legal appeal pending to join his wife there. He was preoccupied only with her:

Teza (from Iran):
I think, for me, I should try the legal way to get to the UK. My wife sent an application for me, for a family reunion, 35 days ago. I don't like my thinking here. It's messy. I am here waiting for this process. I don't know how long this process is. The lawyer says two weeks to six months. But then two weeks ago, a UK MP came here with some people, and I asked them, and they told me two to three months; but I don't know.

My family in Iran, they don't know I am here, but

they know I am safe. I talk to my wife every day on the phone. It's too hard. I am standing by for the visa – every day I check the email. Maybe they will reject the application. Maybe, I don't know.

I haven't thought about what I would do in the UK. It's just that my mind is busy just to find my wife and to look at her.

Teza did, though, describe, like almost every author, one very difficult aspect of 'Jungle' life: the mentally and emotionally confusing and disturbing effects of living with the hardships and uncertainties of the camp. His thinking, as he characterises it above, was 'messy'.

In Teza's accounts of his photo portfolio, the desolation and dangers of the camp were also apparent:

Teza (from Iran):
The street with the church in it is the main place to take a shower. I am not there often. It is not beautiful.

One to two months ago, two houses caught on fire. It started with one candle. That made a fire. One month ago, behind the church, there was another fire. It was bad. I don't know if people were hurt.

For other authors, too, coming to Europe, let alone the UK, had not been their original plan. Being in Calais meant little to them. Shikeb was, as we heard in Chapters 1 and 2, sent to Europe by his mother; he did not want to be there. Because of his employment with US and allied forces, his bad experiences in France, and his professional training in English, he was trying to reach the UK. But he was

FIGURE 3.9
The main street in the 'Jungle'.
Photo by Teza (from Iran).

more concerned about what he had lost in leaving his own country. His account of camp life was short and returned all the time to his mother, and his life in Afghanistan:

Shikeb (from Afghanistan):
Now I have come into the 'Jungle'. This is my story. Sometimes I try to do something good for my life; but life used to be so sweet. I can't do this. I am so tired of this 'Jungle' life. I don't know what I am doing here. I would not be here if my mother had not told me to go to another country. What am I doing here, mum? I tell her, 'Mum, everything is good here.' I don't want

to speak to her. Why did she tell me, 'You go'? She bought me a house, everything; then she told me to go to another country. She is living with my sister now in Afghanistan. I am not happy with my mum.

I don't remember how long I have been here; I think four months. I had two friends in France, but they took everything from me – my trousers, jacket, some English books I had bought. Now I don't have that many friends. Some people are good, some are bad, and I don't know who's good and who's bad.

Sometimes when people are around I am quiet; I don't know what to do. Life with my family and my mum was so sweet, so good. But okay, this is my life; God is writing my life.

I call myself Shikeb in this story, because this is the name my father wanted to call me. But the name I like best is another one, the one I use every day: the one my mother gave me.

Do you think that the son is the enemy of his mother, or the mother is the enemy of her son? Sons are the enemies of their mothers, because if there are four pieces of bread between five, the mother says, 'I am not hungry', and because they grow up and go far away. But I think it is more the second one. Why did she make me leave? I know she wanted me to be safe. But she did a terrible thing to me. I had a happy life with her and my sister and now I have nothing. I have written a poem for my mother, saying how much I now recognise her goodness and beauty.

Reframing the 'Jungle'

For many of the authors of this book, people's lives in the 'Jungle' also need to be shown as resistant, constructive, creative – even transformative.

Babak (from Iran):
It is me who is making his world and no one and nothing can help it better than myself.

All it takes, is to believe in myself and confront my fears!

I remember during the first week that I arrived in the Calais camp (the 'Jungle'), after two horrible nights, I went to the Dome, a place where physical exercises were being conducted by volunteers. People were singing songs and everyone was going on the platform in turn. I always hated my voice. I had never sung before, but that night, I went up, closed my eyes and sang a song. Everyone enjoyed it, and I won a prize. I realised it was easy. For doing this, I only needed to believe in myself and break the fear inside me.

All the troubles and fears we create for ourselves are the products of our thoughts and it is us who make demons out of things. In reality, life is beautiful. We make it difficult; we build walls and are scared of facing them. If we believe in ourselves, we can make impossible things possible and prove that there is nothing impossible!

We have the power to achieve what we want. You can be a great footballer, a fantastic actor, perhaps a successful vendor or even a good writer! I managed to

receive a prize although I had a horrible voice.
All it takes is to close our eyes to our fears.

Everyday humanity

Ali took pictures of Friday prayers:

Ali (from Iran):
It's a beautiful day. All the praying shows that they
have hope in God.

Shikeb photographed his phone, which as for most residents
was an extremely important means of communicating with
family, friends, volunteers, and legal and other services, and
of finding out about events in the outside world.

Despite their negative accounts of camp violence, Zeeshan
Javid and Zeeshan Imayat, who are cousins, took, more
positively, photos of friends, and of how the camp is at
night, when only residents see it, as well as of Calais itself:

Zeeshan Javid (from Pakistan)
That is 'Jungle' people's life. So I was thinking about
the life of the people in the camp and so I took that
picture of the containers. I wanted to show life in the
night time. And I also wanted to show the shop where
we buy things to cook.

FIGURE 3.10
Friday prayers. Photo by Ali (from Iran).

FIGURE 3.11
The containers at night. Photo by Zeeshan Javid (from Pakistan).

FIGURE 3.12
This is the shopkeeper; I know him. Photo by Zeeshan Javid (from Pakistan).

FIGURE 3.13
Here, people are sitting outside and talking. The sun is good.
Photo by Zeeshan Imayat (from Pakistan).

Zeeshan Imayat also took a series of pictures showing everyday social life around the containers:

Zeeshan Imayat (from Pakistan):
I stay in the container camp. If someone from the camp wants to visit, they will have their fingerprints taken to go into the container camp. It is just for them to check who is coming in and who is coming out.

Often, we are just sitting outside of the containers here when the weather is good. We are outside, sitting and reading and learning – just letting time pass. We are all together and we are talking about something: 'How's your life?' 'How are European people?' British people are better than European. British people are good. I see all European people. Now I have seen it in Belgium, in France, and in Italy also; they will ignore you. They give asylum but the people, not the government, people – French, Belgium, Italian – they will ignore you. I see all European people because I have been to several places. English people they will help you, but European people, they will ignore you.

Teddy pictured and described the normality and commonality of activities around the church, a major landmark:

Teddy (from Eritrea):
Sometimes I am tired, not because of trying in the night to get to the UK, but because I have to stay up all night to guard the church, because of fires. We take turns to do this; we are ten of us each night.

FIGURE 3.14
Finding phone reception. Photo by Zeeshan Imayet.

FIGURE 3.15
Inside the church. Photo by Teddy (from Eritrea).

FIGURE 3.16
Making tea. Photo by Babak (from Iran).

Babak also produced a number of images showing people's care for their living environments:

Babak (from Iran):
I took a picture of a man sitting in his chair in front of the container. It is sunny and he is looking at the sky; he made tea. It is his home. I think he lives alone here. He cares about his house. I drink tea with him sometimes. He is from Sudan.

What people are doing is they are building a city, they are trying to keep this as a city, trying to keep life here. It doesn't look like life. This is all they have. A group of volunteers wrote 'lieu de vie' [living spaces] on many buildings because then the police saw that people were living here and did not demolish it.

FIGURE 3.17
In a really bad place, there is a beautiful place like this.
It's behind the dome. Photo by Habibi (from Afghanistan).

Finally, Habibi used his portfolio to show a number of positive aspects of his 'Jungle' life:

Habibi (from Afghanistan):
The pictures show my view of the 'Jungle'. The whole set is a good view of the 'Jungle'. In one place, there is a small outside 'room' and table, a very good place for visiting.

There is also one scenic place in the 'Jungle' – there are no residents there. Up to now, they really don't know about this place. Sometimes I am just going there for a half hour, one hour, just sitting and relaxing. It's the most relaxed place in the 'Jungle'. There's a good view. It's a nice place, no sounds of anything. There are fish around, and some people come to fish here. It's a nice quiet place. I have taken photos of this place, and exhibited them in the Dome. Here, I can put my fingers in the water. Even when I was on my way coming here, to take photos, I was thinking for like five minutes before about it. This place is so nice and you will be like, 'This is a piece of the "Jungle"?'

Beauty in the 'Jungle'

Like Habibi, a number of other authors pictured and wrote about finding beauty in the camp. Haris was unusual among authors: once he had arrived, he started his own shop, followed quickly by a restaurant. This gave him a special vantage point:

Haris (from Pakistan):
In one photo, there is a car coming, I saw that there was a very good view. I like the light. It is a rainy night. I was sitting outside the restaurant and I felt like capturing the moment, so that is why I took the picture. I find it very beautiful. I like it.

There is a lot of beauty in the camp. Beauty depends on the mind and the eyes through which you look at things. You can capture good images as well as bad images. It depends on you. I want to give a good image.

Mani (from Iran):
You need a fire to get warm, and at this time we haven't got anything to do. A lot of people in the 'Jungle' make a fire; sitting around the fire, it is great to tell something together. Mostly my fireside friends are

FIGURE 3.18
Rainy night. Photo by Haris (from Pakistan).

Sudanian, but some of them are Iranian. I am Iranian.
We all speak different languages; we can't understand
each other. It is amazing some people make connections together, maybe with English.

The main street in the 'Jungle' is also beautiful for
me. I pass that way a lot, a lot, some thousand times.
This area for us has not a very good feeling, not good
memories. We all have dreams and wishes. But we can
add some beauty to this place.

It is not a good memory, because 99 per cent don't
want to be here. Sometimes we can find something
beautiful or interesting in this place. Sometimes in a
place you hate you can find something interesting and
beautiful. I find a beauty in this place.

Learning in the 'Jungle'

Finally, authors produced extensive descriptions of the help and support they gained in the camp, and of the initiatives that they and others took. Teza noted some positive factors in relation to his photographs of camp facilities:

> *Teza (from Iran):*
> I have made friends here; it's good, yes; but my mind is too busy. All people here, all have the stress. I visit all the places here. Nine o'clock breakfast, I come to Salam[5], to go to the toilet, sometimes to shower, and then come to here, then to take a lunch and then come here again. Today, I was at Jungle Books Library for more than eight hours. Sometimes I sleep there. Sometimes I learn some English. I go there every day.
>
> And the Good Chance Centre is a good place. Every time they have fun shows for people here. Theatre and music. I like to go there.

Shikeb, too, was sometimes positive in describing his experiences and his own contributions in the camp:

> *Shikeb (from Afghanistan):*
> When I first came here, someone gave me a tent and blankets, and then I went to one of the restaurants. When I came back, everything had gone. I went to the restaurant again. I was sad and didn't know where to sleep. Peter was there and he came to me and asked me what was wrong. I told him that I had

---

5 Salam was a voluntary association providing services to camp residents: http://www.associationsalam.org/

FIGURE 3.19
Jungle Books Library. Photo by Teza (from Iran).

lost everything, and I didn't know where I would sleep that night. He told me, 'Come with me.' I told him, 'I don't have anything.' He said, 'I have everything, come.' He gave me a place to sleep. He's a good friend, a good person. He calls me 'Doctor'. I know about 21 different illnesses, and I tell people if they have to go and get vaccines.

Shikeb also took many photos of the camp school where he had been volunteering from soon after he arrived:

In the school, I made and put up this picture. I want to keep busy all the time. If I stop, I may start to think.

Zeeshan Javid wrote about the value of the University of East London short course, taught by the editors of this book and running in some of the camp schools; he enrolled on the course, almost as soon as he reached the camp:

FIGURE 3.20
Life's story is like shirt buttons. Photo by Shikeb (from Afghanistan).

Zeeshan Javid (from Pakistan):
It is important for me with the UEL certificate. I think
about my future. When I meet French people, in the
future, I have this document. Maybe I will find a good
job. Maybe they will help me in the future. I want to
study maths. My cousin and I were studying together
in Pakistan. We want to become engineers. Right now,
we just want safety. Back in Pakistan, we have a lot of
problems. When they give me French documents or
any European documents I will tell them, I need documents just for that; for my safety and for my family's
safety. My family are still in Pakistan but if I have the
documents they will also come. Now, we need more
help but not everyone is ready to help.

Haris described the value of his own project – his shop,
which later became a restaurant:

Haris (from Pakistan):
This is my restaurant, the Blue Lake, where I am
serving people tea, food and coffee. In the beginning, I did not think about opening a restaurant. To
start with, I built a small shop but then I realised that
people need a lot. They need some food, some fresh
tea, coffee and all these things – so I started to build
this restaurant.

Some authors told more general stories about the positive
influences of the 'Jungle'. Habibi described learning a great
deal in the camp:

FIGURE 3.21
The Blue Lake restaurant. Photo by Haris (from Pakistan).

Habibi (from Afghanistan):
If you had a look around in the Jungle, you would
know it's hard to have hopes here. In here, I dream
of England. I take pictures of the landscape. I use the
images to say something about the beauty of England.
If you can find a nice place in this jungle, then imagine
what England must be like! When I first came here,
the first night, I was crying. I had no place to sleep. I
walked around in the 'Jungle' to find a place to sleep
and I found a camp kitchen in between some trees.
It was covered but had no walls. I slept there for one
night. When the morning came, I went and talked to
people, greeted them with 'Salam'. I was shown where
I could get some blankets and now I have a tent close

153

to the library. I started living. People in the 'Jungle' have different stories about their journeys and their lives in here, but I train myself in here, in how to face difficulties. Now, if you take me anywhere in the world, if you put me in a jungle, I will be able to live in there. Everywhere. Because I trained myself in here. Three months' training is a lot. I only had a pair of pants and one pair of shoes when I arrived. Now I work, I collect things and I have a good tent I can sleep in. A very good tent. I prefer my tent over a caravan. I have three blankets in my tent, two blankets beneath me and one above me. It is very good, I am warm and sleep without problems.

Looking at the positive aspects of 'Jungle' life from a more collective stance, Refugees' Voice wrote a series of diary entries about how people in the 'Jungle' were organising effectively to meet their own needs, starting in late 2015:

Refugees' Voice (from Afghanistan):
December 2015: We are peaceful humans currently living in Calais's 'Jungle', 6,000 plus. We appreciate all humanitarian support from volunteers but we want to find political way to get to the UK safely. We are not terrorists but we are the victims of war and terrorism which has been started by terrorists and the USA along with support of European countries. We want to have respect and dignity with a stable life and solidarity. Humans of Calais haven't left their countries of their own free will; it's by force and persecution. Currently the police violence is increasing day by day. French police are using tear gas, water cannons,

beating people. Earlier on, I found out from the newspaper that the mayor of Calais is calling on the army to intervene in the 'Jungle' instead of the police.

January 2016: Refugees of Calais are peace lovers. It's the refugees and volunteers who have made the Calais 'Jungle' so amazing. And their amazing contributions have given a great structure … From nothing.

Finally, Africa, despite his earlier negative account of the camp, also gave perhaps the most positive account of what it meant for him in his early time there – an account affected by very specific experiences of UK and French volunteers – not shared by all authors or residents – as well as of the multinational residents:

Africa (from Sudan):
Do you want to know, 'Why do you want to go to the UK?' I will answer that question. I have been here for three months, in this wonderful world, the 'Jungle'. Really, it is wonderful. Because of the people inside, they are wonderful. You can see many nations, saying, 'Hi, hello', in different languages. You can see in their eyes that they respect you, but they can't say that to you. Even from their eyes you can tell if they want something; sometimes they are looking for a translator. Or yourself; sometimes you are asking someone, 'Please translate, if you need it.' We are able to talk even in silence. You can find what you want. Someone sees someone who is cold. Maybe he will give you his blanket: 'Take this, you are colder than me.' You can find the real kind of human being here. That is making

all these people real people.

Since I came here I haven't encountered French volunteers. Maybe one, maybe two. Compare it to the number of British volunteers. All these people, they come from England and they support and they are a real help. You see volunteers who stay here for two months and never go to their home. Just because they want to help people who have no help; because of humanity. Also because of how people treat us. In here, there is no difference between black and white. They respect you because you are human. This is the life I want, this is a dignified life. Every single day I spend in here makes me want to go the UK even more, because I discover and get to know more about that place. The French police will spray gas in your eyes, sometimes they will kick you in the stomach, sometimes they will beat you with sticks. You would think they are respected people. (Sometimes they keep people two weeks, even five weeks without anything, just because they are refugees. We do not see anything of France that make us want to stay here.)

You won't meet anyone here upsetting you. People will greet you and welcome you. That is what makes this a wonderful place. I don't have good neighbours in here, I have good brothers. I have brothers from Syria, Eritrea, Sudan, Kurdistan, Afghanistan, Iraq, Egypt. Six thousand people, those are my brothers. I am a rich man. Because of that I sleep in safety. I can eat with anyone in here. I ask them and they ask me, 'Please come here, eat with us.' Do you know why? Not because of money, no. Because of respect. Respect with a little smile. You can do everything here, everything. Because they are looking for respect. Give respect, take respect. Not like outside in the city: 'Give me something and I will give you something.'

You can try this. Go anywhere in the 'Jungle', say 'Hi', and you will hear, 'Hi, please come on in.' You will find people saying, 'Hi, hi my brother', and inviting you in. It is because of this, that I find it wonderful. What I told you about my dream of being useful for the people: I can be that here, all the time. I can help them. I can arrange something. I can ask for food for them. That makes me useful in here. Because of that, I find this place wonderful.

I find happiness here. How many people find true happiness? How will you pay to find happiness? How will you pay? How much? I think I find happiness in here. Real happiness. I am happy. If I go to the centre of Calais, to take a rest, one or two hours later I will miss the 'Jungle' and come back here. Because I think I belong in this place. If I go to the UK, I will try to help the people here, from there. Until my last days in my life I will try to help people anywhere. Anywhere.

The next chapter explores further these ambiguities of living in the 'Jungle', in relation to longer-term residence, 'trying' to get to the UK, and building community feeling and institutions in the camp.

CHAPTER 4

Living in and leaving the 'Jungle': Connecting, longing and trying to leave

From the preceding chapters, we already know that the 'Jungle' was only one stop, a temporary settlement, on longer journeys that, for many, have not yet ended. However, residents sometimes stayed for longer periods due to various circumstances, of which we will hear in this chapter. What will be evident is that leaving the 'Jungle' was a process that rarely happened overnight. Authors tell of the activities, work, communities and long-term connections they established while staying in the camp. We will also hear about the many and often dangerous attempts to reach the UK and about people's sometimes ambiguous thoughts about leaving the 'Jungle', a place to which some authors came to feel connected.

In the previous chapter, Babak told how he claimed asylum in France during detention, after a failed attempt to leave for the UK. Waiting for an asylum claim to be processed in France, as in Babak's case, is one example of why some asylum seekers ended up staying in the 'Jungle' for longer periods. This chapter opens with Babak continuing his account of what led him into a long-term stay in Calais:

FIGURE 4.1

This is the fence. It is close to the car ferry and to the place where I first was arrested with my friends with the fake passport. We tried going by bus. This place will always remind me of that day. Photo by Babak (from Iran).

Babak (from Iran):

They took me to the detention centre for one month in France. The detention centre is really bad. They were pressuring me by repeatedly saying, 'They want to deport you.' I said 'OK, I will put my finger-print here', but they didn't explain what was going to happen when asking for asylum in the deten-tion centre. They don't give you anything when you do that, no papers, no home and no money. I think they cheated me, but I am trying to fight the situa-tion now. I could have waited and asked for asylum at the asylum office when I got out of the detention centre – that would be normal. They force you to ask for asylum in the detention centre without advising you. I think they cheated me because they didn't tell me what was going to happen afterwards. The police transferred me to the detention centre as if I had done some bad criminal job. I came here the same way as all refugees. They came illegally and I came illegally. I don't know why they didn't tell me about the consequences of asking for asylum in the detention centre. When you go to the interview with the police, they don't care about you; they just try to reject you. They told me, 'You have a big case, you have a lot of proof, you have the report and the text you write and you can ask for asylum here, it is really faster and better for you. You have a good chance to get accepted.' It wasn't like this.

The detention centre is in Calais, two hours' walking from the camp. After twenty days, they told me I was rejected. They transferred me to a centre in Paris where I stayed for two days. In total, I stayed for one month in the detention centre and on the last day, they transferred me to the police because they were trying to clean Calais.

The last day I asked the association in Paris[1] and they told me that I would be free today, and that I could ask for an appeal about the decision. They told me that it was a big mistake to ask for asylum in the detention centre. They said I could go to a place in Paris to ask for an appeal. I went there and I explained my situation. They said I should come back in one

---

1 A visiting social worker from an association that provides legal advice informed Babak about his rights and options while he was in detention.

FIGURE 4.2
This is a very horrible place here, but people are living.
Photo by Babak (from Iran).

week. I didn't have a place to stay and I didn't want to stay on the street in Paris, so I decided to go to Calais. I found a legal association centre here and wrote my appeal. Now I am waiting for the processing of my case.

I just want to explain that there are good things about the 'Jungle' and bad things, a lot of them, here. The good and bad things are all close to each other. I think that most of the people who are living here have dreams of England. They're living in this bad situation, but I think that everywhere we are free; everywhere we can be free. This is a very horrible place, but they are living, so I think there is no difference between England, France, or any other country – they can live anywhere. I think they are wasting their time here in the 'Jungle'. It's hell here, but we are living.

Connecting

While longing for other lives and opportunities during extended stays, residents did not wait passively. Refugees and non-residents collaborated around daily social and cultural activities and they worked to provide and distribute basics such as food, clothing, tents and blankets. Many authors worked with voluntary associations and some initiated their own projects, often with help from outside volunteers bringing donated material to the camp or providing their labour. Residents had the advantage of knowing the camp communities and their needs from within and some became initiators of humanitarian work, like the author Africa, who first worked independently, initiating charity distribution, and then later collaborating with voluntary organisations. Working long hours as a volunteer, he, like residents in similar positions, obtained a caravan to live in. In Chapter 1, Africa described his thoughts about being a useful and responsible person and how he grew up wanting to be like Bruce Lee; here he continues these thoughts:

> *Africa (from Sudan):*
> When I was trying to follow my dream of being useful to other people, I mentioned Bruce Lee – he is an ethical person. He protects persons who are weak. I like being a person who protects the weak. Maybe now I am another kind of Bruce Lee. I try to protect the

refugees. They fight a difficult fight. Sometimes you can choose; I want to do this. Not that you should fight. You should help. You should try to do your best. To be useful, to be a man. You are not a man because you are strong or because of your acts. You should put the weak before the strong in a bad time, not just in a good time. This will show you who is bad and who is good.

I will do my best to help people. The best solution is ideally where a man helps as much as he can: 'God helps his servant as long as he helps his brother.' This is a hadith of the Prophet, peace be upon him, and he cannot be faulted, he is right. The Prophet said that the best of men are the ones who are most useful to the people. The Lord, God, he promised that, 'When you help your brothers, I will help you.'

I didn't pay anything for this caravan. It has been brought here to help me. I wear clothes. I didn't buy them. My life is good; I am in a good situation. Eating, drinking, wearing clothes, sleeping well – that is all I need. I am in a better situation than the millions of people that sometimes can't find anything to eat at all, that cannot find a place to sleep. I am good.

Some authors posted diary entries on Facebook. Using social media, Refugees' Voice, introduced in the previous chapter, and Riaz Ahmad, who moved out of the camp but kept volunteering and remained strongly connected to the 'Jungle', addressed both residents and people from outside the camp. Both authors encouraged others with their reports of humanitarian work and sought to strengthen collaborations in the 'Jungle' and between its communities:

Riaz (from Pakistan):

26 March 2016: May Allah bring you lots of happiness and joy on Easter Day. May Allah give you a long life so you can celebrate Easter a hundred times. Happy Easter to every one of my Christian friends.

3 April 2016: An Afghan family with two kids arrived in the camp last night and they just spent one night at some place in the 'Jungle'. They desperately need a warm place. If you know someone or have a spare caravan in the warehouse or in England, do let me know please. We should give them a proper and warm place, please.

5 July 2016: The holy month of Ramadan is over tonight and Muslims will celebrate the Eid ul-Fitr festival. This is a very important religious holiday, so I am sending Eid ul-Fitr Mubarak greetings to everyone in advance from the bottom of my heart.

26 August 2016: I should help others because I am. I should help because it's the right thing to do. I will help them because our lives here are important and equally so are other people's lives. It's the decent, human and most natural way to want to behave when others are suffering. I will help because we all survived as one human race. We all are or could be friends or relatives!

Refugees' Voice (from Afghanistan):
5 November 2015: Today I met volunteers who were trying to fix the heating system for refugees' houses. This caught my eye, and I want to share and support their efforts. I'm so happy that we still have many nice people who are supporting refugees. I just wanted to share and appreciate all your hard work and the time you spend in the 'Jungle' with us.

6 November 2015: We are warmly welcoming all volunteers and refugees for traditional Afghan food and live traditional Afghan music in the Ashram Kitchen in Calais, with the support of the Ashram Kitchen. We have organised an Afghan team who is going to be in charge of the kitchen on Saturday 7th November, Inshallah!

Under the alias 'Refugees' Voice', and via his Facebook page with the same name, this author wanted to gather and represent the voices of residents and communities in the 'Jungle'. In the following, he explains why and how he attempted to give help and to improve communication and organisation, including by helping create a residents' council:

Refugees' Voice:
When I was in Calais, I was helping people and doing quite a lot of translations if anyone needed some information or some help. Because of my language skills, I could communicate with everyone and I knew people across all communities. I always wanted to reach people and help them if they wanted me to. The people building the shelters would ask me, 'Could you

tell the others how to build the shelter?', or 'Can you tell them how to do this or that?', 'Where can I find the blankets?' 'How can I do this or that?' I remember late September when I arrived in the 'Jungle', I asked somebody 'Where can I get a blanket?' And he said, 'There, in the shop.' But I did not have money so I could not buy it. I had to ask people where I could find a place to get a blanket. Finally, I found the place where I could get a free blanket and a tent. I realised that there are so many people in need and I also realised that there are other people, like me, in the 'Jungle', who are trying to help other people. I met an Afghan guy who was also trying to help and I met people from other communities and I thought, 'Why are we working separately?' Then we created a community representation and I created the Facebook page 'Refugees' Voice'. I was trying to help and raise the rights of refugees. Since most did not want to show their faces, I created the page to speak their voices.

Personally, I was not the representative of any community, but I was more interested in the process of making unity and gathering all the communities. I lived in the UK for so long and developed language and communication skills, so I thought I would be good at that. I also knew about the rights of refugees and had social abilities. I was doing a radio show called 'Hopeshow' on the 'Jungle' radio and I was trying to help in the library as well. At the same time, I was working with unaccompanied minors and Citizens UK. In those ways, I was trying to put more strength into the community.

FIGURE 4.3

Food ready to serve in Haris's restaurant. Photo by Haris (from Pakistan).

Refugees have, sometimes in collaboration with non-residents, opened restaurants and shops in the 'Jungle', each serving food from one of the many different cultures represented here. The restaurants are, apart from their main function of serving food, places for watching TV and charging phones, which are people's vital link with home, families, lawyers and help from voluntary associations outside the camp. Residents with different nationalities and from different communities meet and talk here, making camp restaurants important spaces for communities to grow and develop.

Haris (from Pakistan):
The restaurant didn't look like it does now at first. I

extended it three times to make room for the customers coming here. I received help from people working with a French voluntary organisation in the camp. One of them brought us the plastic, wood material, even plates, cylinders and benches.

Back home, I was a student. Without money, you can't survive. Before, here in the 'Jungle', the government didn't provide you with anything or give you food. You had to ensure your own food, your own clothes and shoes, everything. Before, I think one year ago, it was very hard for the refugees. I arrived here in January 2015.

I think this place is important for people because lots of people are coming here, charging their mobile phones, get together, discuss with each other and get food and drinks as well. People are from different communities. Iraqis, Syrian, Eritrean, Sudanese, Pakistani, Afghani people come here. All mixed together.

Some English speakers are, due to language barriers, less likely to interact with helpful French organisations, friendly French people and even helpful police. France may then come to be associated with violent policing, ultra-right politics and an unfriendliness that contrasts with the highly valued support and care experienced from other nationalities, as Ali Bajdar explains:

Ali Bajdar (from Iraq):
When I go to England, I want to help other people. One thing you can do is to smile and be kind. To me, receiving a smile is more important than receiving things. Clothes and shoes, such things are good, of

course, but in the end all you need is people who smile and are kind towards you. When you feel that other people consider you an animal, you cannot live together. When you hear people telling you not to worry, that things are hard but will get better, it is different. It gives you energy. When I go to the village, it seems like the French pretend that they don't understand what I am saying and that they don't want to talk to me. I am not saying that all French are like that, but I have friends from England, Switzerland, Germany, Belgium and Denmark who come here and spend their time helping and I rarely meet any French people.

Belonging – 'We are all human'

Authors emphasise the importance of giving and receiving support and engaging in active 'human' lives despite living in what they refer to as a 'Jungle'. Some describe how they learn a new language, dance, play, maintain cultural and religious traditions – or are inspired to try out new ones – and how they share their stories and dreams with each other. In this process, friendships and a sense of belonging develop that reaches beyond national borders, cultural differences and language:

> Mani (from Iran):
> His name is Reza, my Sudanese neighbour. I remember when I arrived in the 'Jungle', I thought all African persons were so dangerous and cruel because we have no Africans in my country, and I had no connection with them. My imaginings about African people were from the Hollywood movies. The first

FIGURE 4.4
The 'Jungle' church wall. Photo by Mani (from Iran).

night I slept in my single tent in their area, all the night I couldn't sleep because of the fear. But now I think the best people in the 'Jungle' are the Sudanese. Now I trust them more than my country's people.

The first day, at the first moment when I came into the 'Jungle', I went to the church. Not to pray, I just thought, 'Here is more safe.' Now, as I walk around that wall, I can hear the sounds of the psalms in a strange language, 'Eritrean'. Before the 'Jungle', never had I heard that.

I can hear the sound of life in this land. Not just the voice of Eritrean hip hop music from the night clubs in the street. Because this street is full of humans with many hopes, dreams. I don't know whether, when they follow their dreams, they are doing right or wrong. It doesn't matter, we are alive; all living humans follow their dreams. Maybe sometimes in the wrong way.

Around the fire in the cold of the Calais winter we

FIGURE 4.5
Night falls. Photo by Mani (from Iran).

will be warm, not from the fire, from our imaginary
stories, bluffs, lies, jokes and heroic stories about our
tries. I don't think about what is true or false. But
those will warm us. I like the 'Jungle' nights. I am
feeling that the 'Jungle' in the night just belongs to
us. Belongs to us refugees. In the nights, especially
at midnight. You can't see any volunteers, police, or
journalists. Just refugees. I am feeling more safe, more
comfortable at these times.

Ali Bajdar (from Iraq):
I stay in a tent with people who have become my
friends. In the night, we go to our tent and talk about
the future and about our plans and dreams. We talk
about the past, about life back in Iraq and about the
war. You want to ask, 'What did you see?', 'What did

FIGURE 4.6
Making art in the Dome – the Good Chance Centre.
Photo by Babak (from Iran).

you do?', 'What do you think about now and what do
you think about for the future?'

Babak (from Iran):
The media they record people trying to get to the UK
and they show people trying to make trouble, people
hitting the cars, jumping on the cars. It is not like this.
Some people they are living here, some people they are
studying here, they are going to school. Some people
they have nothing to say. For example, like me, I don't
go and try to get to the UK, I am just living here.
They show these people in the media. They show this
bad image of people fighting with the police. When
people are seeing all of these really bad things in the
media, they think we are not human beings, they

think we are violent. They think a lot of bad things and get a really bad image. When they come to visit the camp, they see that it is not like this, they see they are all just humans.

The people from 'Care4Calais' are always trying to make some entertainment for people. They distribute clothes, food and also they arrange spaces for football and volleyball, they are very active. It is really good that they are here because the people in the camp, apart from clothes and food, they also need entertainment like education and sport – they need more of this.

Volunteers also arranged events specifically for women, as Safia describes here:

Safia (from Afghanistan):
'Beauty Day', organised by the Blue Bus, is good. It is good because you can have your nails polished and your eyebrows done. People come for massage, nail-polish, for makeup, everything. One time, someone came and I got my hair done, together with another woman.

Learning

Many seek the opportunity to learn English or French at the schools in the 'Jungle' where lessons for both children and adults are offered on a daily basis. Some prepare for future education or practice social interaction in what might become their new home country. For some, living in the 'Jungle' also becomes an education in different ways of living, as the next authors explain:

FIGURE 4.7
*This is in the morning with the people from Care4Calais.
Photo by Babak (from Iran).*

Muhammad (from Syria):
One day, I saw Mustafa reading a book and asked him. 'Where is that from?' He said. 'From Jungle Books Library.' A few days later, I went with Mustafa and Anur and another man to see the Jungle Books Library. Anur used to attend English lessons there, so I decided to have a look. We went a little early and there was a French lesson. I decided to attend that class, maybe I could learn some words in French. The teacher was a French man, he knew Arabic and English as well. This man would later improve my view of French people and Europeans. He was a handsome, kind and smart man; he was really the kind of man that you can hardly find in Western countries.

Because we knew nothing about the French language, he invited us to return next day at 3pm. when there would be a class for beginners. After the class finished, I wanted to leave, but Anur insisted on me staying for the English class. It started at 5pm. To my surprise it was a conversation class, which all the people who wanted to improve their English attended to have conversations with others, especially with English-speaking volunteers.

For me, Calais was the first place where I actually used the English language. However, in the class, I met an Italian girl. She was studying in London and came here for the weekend as a volunteer. She spoke the English language clearly and knew French as well. She was like an angel. She had an innocent, beautiful face and she seemed very educated. I met her also in the next class next day. The conversation class was really useful for me, not just to improve my language, but also to get to know other people and cultures.

Shikeb (from Afghanistan):
I didn't know any English before I came here, but now I want to learn. I have practiced for four months. I have a dictionary in my phone; I try to learn with this. In the school, I sometimes help the teachers arranging the books and sometimes I read. The teachers don't know my language, so I use my phone for translation. I have worked in one of the schools, but I never wanted money for that. I think knowledge should be pure and beautiful, never for money.

Habibi (from Afghanistan):

When I came here, I stopped eating animals. Why should we kill poor animals? I learned many things in here, in the 'Jungle'. When I came here, I met British people who weren't eating meat. I asked them why and they said, 'Why should we kill the poor animals?' Believe me, I have learned from those people. If you offered me chicken, or anything like that, I would not want to eat it. I just love animals – why would we want to eat them? They also love to live!

My journey changed me. Before, I was something else. Before I came here, I had no mercy, I was acting violently. I was killing and eating cows, now I wouldn't kill a chicken. I was working at a hospital as a translator and living as a rich guy, spending money every day. I did not eat at home, I just went to a hotel and ate there and I often went on tours with my friends. I spent a lot of money on that. My mum was complaining, 'Why are you spending your money on these things?' I said, 'Mum, I am working, I am earning money, this is my money, let me spend it', and she didn't object.

Something happened when I started travelling. I became a stronger man, I learned how to face difficulties. From when I left home and up until now, I have experienced so many difficulties and dangers. I have been beaten many times. Now, I know how to defend myself. I have been living in the 'Jungle' for three months. I have no money and I am fine. I am spending my time in here and it is fine.

Longing

Majid (from Iran):
I like reading self-help books a lot. It's important to keep a positive attitude – it's easy to lose that here.

Africa (from Sudan):
I've been very busy in the 'Jungle', and now I am doing less; I want to rest.

Keeping engaged when staying long-term is a challenge, especially for those dealing with or developing medical health issues. Nightly attempts to leave may disrupt a daily rhythm. The weather can be rough and cold. It is muddy, dirty and indoor spaces are few. Thoughts and worries about home and the future at times hinder focus and concentration. Some manage to stay in contact with friends and family and benefit from regular contact with loved ones, though financial limits and a lack of signal and wi-fi in the camp complicates communication. To some camp residents, time spent in the camp feels like a waste of their potential. Accordingly, a focus on camp activities is sometimes considered the best use of their time or a necessity to escape despair and longing momentarily.

Zeeshan Imayat (from Pakistan):
When the weather is good, maybe after four or five o'clock, everyone is outside of their house. They are playing something, for example, football or cricket. They will play something just for relaxation. The problem is that we are alone here and it is a boring

life, it is a prison life. No mother, no father, no brother, no sister. We miss that, so we are coming outside just for relaxation and we are playing something.

Life in the 'Jungle' is a very boring life; when your mind is not busy, it wanders back home. You remember your home. When you are busy with something, being busy somewhere, it is good. When you are thinking too much about home or about Europe that is a problem.

We have the problem in the 'Jungle' that we have no money. We can't just call to Pakistan, Sudan and everywhere from France or the UK because it is very expensive. But when you have internet or wi-fi, it is very easy to call people at home. Everyone comes here, they connect to wi-fi, they will call, and they will send messages. I text my brother, who is in Australia, and my father, who is in Pakistan.

Teddy (from Eritrea):
When we stay here, we are thinking all the time about our country and our family. We are spending time without benefit. We are young, we are energetic, but we don't get a learning opportunity or a job opportunity in this situation.

I play football with my friends. Before, there were tents where we play, but now they are demolished. Everyone is keen to watch Euro 2016, but for the European Champions' League, we had to pay €2 per game to watch in a café and it was very crowded with no space.

I have lots of medical books in my house; I try to read them but I am often tired. I have made my house

FIGURE 4.8
This is the kitchen in the camp. It is called 'Calais' and there is wi-fi for free. Photo by Zeeshan Imayat (from Pakistan).

as good as I can, considering where I am living.

We are human beings. Sometimes when you are new in a country, it is stressful. When you can contact friends and family by phone, or have them beside you, it reduces the stress. But I am flexible; I can adapt anywhere to the situation: any culture, any language.

Sometimes, if people need to call, we are coming to the ridge, because we are searching for a signal. The ridge is much higher than the surrounding land. Also, if you need to talk with your family about some private things, you would come here. The shelters are very crowded so you cannot talk freely.

FIGURE 4.9

I remember that I took this picture to show how people develop stress, but how, when we play, the stress is already gone. I play football, but this is a picture of my friends playing; some are just watching.
Photo by Teddy (from Eritrea).

Zeeshan Javid (from Pakistan):
When the weather is very cold, we are sitting under the roof in the camp kitchen. We are making a fire. We are missing our families and we talk with friends. We are cooking here, but we can't cook when we have no facilities and no gas. When we have no gas, they give us food in the Jules Ferry Centre one time in 24 hours. When you take this food, you are sick. Every day, you are sick. We cook for ourselves but it is a problem that we have no gas. Every day, we are making a fire. When we talk with the organisations in the camp, we ask them to help us get gas. Sometimes we wait for two or three weeks, and then they tell us that they can't help us because there is no money.

FIGURE 4.10
The ridge. Photo by Teddy (from Eritrea).

It is a problem that we need to have our fingerprints taken when we enter the container part of the camp; it is too much control. But they tell me that the fingerprints is just for the camp, not for any European countries that will give you problems, just for the camp. I believe that.

Mani (from Iran):
Javid speaks with his wife in Iran.

He shows himself as hopeful to her. But me and the Afghan boy, we know this is not true.

I hope she doesn't understand that Javid is telling lies to her.

Everywhere is full of rubbish, but we have to live between it. Maybe because we made it ourselves. Don't worry, after a period of time we are accustomed to it. I try to see the sky when crossing through it. But how can I cross it without looking at it? Some days when I had extra bread, I put it on the rock near my shelter for feeding the birds and it disappeared after some minutes. I was so happy that I was feeding the beautiful birds. But it was strange the birds ate it so fast. One day, I understood that rats ate the bread, not birds. I was feeding the rats and I helped them to grow their population. After some weeks, one night, I saw a rat in my shelter. They had grown so much, and I helped them. Anytime I saw the rats, I remembered the smugglers in the Calais 'Jungle'.

Ali Bajdar (from Iraq):
There are still days where I cannot eat or walk, so I stay in my tent, sometimes for days. I get paracetamol when I go to see the doctor in the camp. That is all they can do for me here. When I moved to Dunkirk, there was no school so I couldn't practice my English anymore. Sometimes there is no food. If I am hungry, I have to wait for the next day. We all have two pairs of shoes here: one pair for the camp and one for going outside. It's because of the mud.

Like the authors above, Refugees' Voice not only reports positive stories from the camp, but also raises awareness of the general and more acute issues in the camp:

Refugees' Voice (from Afghanistan):
30 October 2015: Hundreds of people waiting for the gates of the government-run Jules Ferry Centre to open. The centre houses women and children and

provides some services to other camp residents. The gates are supposed to open at nine. It's 9.28am, but they are still closed. Some are waiting to get a shower; unluckily they have to wait hours to get their turn. Others are waiting for the washroom or for tea. This is the life in the 'Jungle'. It was sorted by 9.30. Everyone had to wait that extra 30 minutes. They need to increase the amount of facilities so people don't wait so long in the queue for taking a shower. Normally, a person has to wait two to three hours to get their turn.

14 November 2015: Fire in the 'Jungle'. It's not the first fire actually, it's the second. Last time it was during the day so luckily, we stopped it from spreading, but this one, we couldn't. It is frightening as kids, families and individuals are living in the 'Jungle' and it's obvious how bad the 'Jungle' life is. Thanks for your support and sincere thoughts. I hope there are changes soon as it's getting colder and colder day by day.

21 November 2015, 1.50am: Another fire in the 'Jungle'. I don't know what's going on; it's horrible and uncontrollable and spreading so fast. I hope everyone will stay safe. A team of refugees is trying to evacuate all tents.

3.24am: Everything has calmed down and it's all under control but the bad news is we have three bad burn injuries. Many volunteers were here with aid for the refugees. Really great work done by them, and it's appreciated by me.

Trying to leave

Even though many remained in the 'Jungle' long-term, they did not accept this living arrangement as a permanent one. They dreamed of better lives and better places and many tried to leave Calais in various ways. When trying to leave, camp residents experienced violent encounters with the French police and occasionally with far-right political activists. The French authorities used all means necessary to control the movement of refugees from Calais to the UK. With the use of tear gas, water cannons, physical assault, arrest and detention, leaving the camp was sometimes described in terms of a fight or a war, sometimes against political parties with violent tendencies towards the camp residents,[2] but most often with the police, even the UK police, and with smugglers:

> *Shikeb (from Afghanistan):*
> I have tried to go to the UK from Calais on lorries and on ferries, but the police always found and attacked me. Once, I could not walk for four days. I went to Dieppe three times to try to get to the UK. The first time, I was sleeping on the street. I was attacked and my head was injured. After two nights, I found some African people and they called me, 'Hey Shikeb, you were living in the "Jungle"!' I said to myself, 'Let's make friends, and besides, they have a tent.' They gave me everything – shoes, trousers, jackets – and they showed me everywhere. We were going to different

2 Reports and audiovisuals by members of Calais Migrant Solidarity and No Borders network presenting and documenting methods of repression available at calaismigrantsolidarity.wordpress.com.

places together; some with food, others where you can shower. Then I found a government-run place where they only want your name – they have beds, food and wi-fi – they were friendly. I think it was for addicts. It was a good place.

I got to the UK, but they arrested me in the car park in Brighton. I was under a lorry on a ship and then I was found in the parking place. I had been holding on under the lorry for ten hours; I was so tired. In that place, there was a lawyer and he took my name. I couldn't even talk, I was so tired. I agreed to go back to France. Then I came back to Calais. I wasn't sure what to do. In the end, I collected some books from the school and returned to Dieppe. I tried to get to the UK once more, this time in the back of someone's car; but the police found me again. There were too many people trying to stay in the addicts' place, and Dieppe had become very strict with refugees – they were driving them out. Smugglers also cost about €7,000–8,000. You can do so much with that money.

It was a big shock to come back and find so much of the 'Jungle' gone after the March eviction. When I came back, I wanted to make sure the school ran properly again. I painted signs; I re-supplied it with things like Sellotape; we restarted all the classes.

If I had got to the UK now, everything would have been fine. I told my mum I was in the UK. When I needed some money to go back to Dieppe and try again, I couldn't ask her, because she would have known that I had lied. Then, my mum's phone didn't work for three months, and I had already sold my phone to travel to Dieppe, trying to get to the UK.

I thought then that I would try to go to another place – maybe Jersey, which might be easier to get to. But first I wanted to spend one, two months making everything work well in the school.

I went to Dieppe a third time and also to a camp near Rouen. This time, I talked with a smuggler. I made an agreement with him. He said, 'Give me €5,000.' I said, 'I don't have that'. He said, '€2,000 is my best offer'. I said, 'I have this much – if you want, try me.' He took the money I had – €500 – and my phone. So he opened a lorry to put me in it. But the police caught me; they were checking more, because people had recently crossed. Then the smuggler went to Paris. I called him: 'Are you coming back so I can try? If not, I want to go to the "Jungle".' I believed him when he said that the time was not good and we should wait six months. Another refugee was in the same position. We tried by ourselves, there in Dieppe and again in Rouen. The smuggler said he would come in six months, but he was just enjoying himself in Paris. The police told me they could do nothing since the payment was illegal. Finally, the smuggler called, he wanted to meet in the 'Jungle'. I went to the place he had said, but he was not at that place and his phone was off. He is claiming asylum in France himself.

Now I am thinking I won't do this again. I don't have family in the UK to help with money for smugglers. I wanted to fight with the smuggler, but I couldn't. I said, 'It's my problem, not his problem. I gave him the money and trusted him.' This time is confusing. If you tell me to claim asylum, I won't. If you point, 'You are wrong', you have three fingers pointing back

at you. I miss my friends who have gone to the UK.
The only way is to try. Trying is not easy. If it was, all
these people here would be in England. This is what
makes people confused; but they are trying, and trying
is good, because you have hope. I am going to try with
another person; we have to be strong and have hope to
do it. Now I am trying from Calais. I might try from
outside Calais again, maybe this time from Belgium
or Paris. I have hope. One day I will cross. Because
there is God, there is hope.

The attempts

Financial constraints for many camp residents place the
'services' of a people-smuggler out of reach and for those
with money it often runs out, as it did for Shikeb. They are
then left with other, often more dangerous and physically
challenging, ways of trying. Depending on their physical
health and mental state, some consider going elsewhere,
or apply for asylum in France. In the following section, we
will hear authors' thoughts about trying to leave with and
without people smugglers and their related experiences.

Teddy (from Eritrea):
We Africans don't have money for smugglers.
  Most of my friends from the camp have gone to
England. Some have gone to Germany. Others have
claimed asylum in France. In the camp, you ask for
information about European countries and then you
decide. I am waiting to see what happens about getting to England. I have a plan: That is why I am here.
We are suffering. When you ask for asylum, you get

food and a place to live. But in the UK, I have friends; even my uncle is there. The language is important too. Here in France I would be starting from zero. Even here, summer to winter to spring, I have survived a lot of seasons. We are strong. We will go anywhere in the UK. Now, we go by foot up to four hours to the border. We are turned back by the police. We can survive anything. Now the situation is bad and there are fewer places to get onto lorries. Some lorry parks have been demolished. If the situation does not improve, I may go elsewhere – Paris or Germany.

Majid (from Iran):
Crossing the border is the important thing, because they are so strict. I heard that when you enter Dunkirk, every smuggler invites you to their shelter; 'Come to us!', because they want to make contact. But I am staying in Calais because it is the nearest place to the UK – less than one hour by ferry. This is also the biggest port with the most ferries, so there are more chances.

I have tried paying smugglers to help me get into trucks – it's difficult. I tried three times so far. It's by chance, whether you can cross. For some people it works the first time, for others it takes twenty times. It's not dangerous, the smugglers are experts. They have been doing this for over ten years. But there are two kinds of smuggler guys; some will take the money and go; for others, it's a long-term business, they would never do that. The smuggler I talked with was recommended to me – he's famous here.

Not everyone has money for smugglers. Many of the people here who have come from African countries do not. They have to do something far more dangerous – stop trucks by putting trees in the road and then get in.

First, I wanted to go with a fake passport. But I heard that my friend doing this was caught at a Greek airport. So he lost all the money he had spent – €4,000. Because of that news, I changed my mind. I thought that I would contact smugglers instead.

Safia (from Afghanistan):
I asked how much it would cost to cross and they said £1,000 per person. Now some people say £5,000. But we don't have too much money. I tried to go alone without my children; I was pregnant at that time. I did not pay anyone – but people said you have to pay if you want to cross. My father-in-law will pay and maybe my cousin will also pay another thousand. Somebody – a friend – took me in the night and I stayed in the car park and I got arrested straight away. Then the police took me to the train station and then to another place, and then I came back. My husband did not try because this would be trouble for the children. I am still trying.

Mani (from Iran):
A furious Eritrean man came to me, shouted, 'Don't take a picture!' He was afraid of the camera, hid his face at my insistence to let me take a picture of him. He has hopes that one day he will be in the UK and nobody will recognise him and know that he was in the Calais 'Jungle'. Me too, I wish I can go to the UK – but I want him to achieve his goal too. He gave me

a strange look. I thought he said to himself, 'He is not looking like a journalist or volunteer. He is from the "Jungle". Why is he taking a picture here?' Maybe he thought I was a spy.

I look at my watch. It's so late. Tonight, like other nights, I have to go and try. The Calais 'Jungle': dark is coming. Day dies but life in the 'Jungle' begins. I should be ready to go to try. Mostafa told me, 'Hurry up; we have to be at 7 in the Kurdish restaurant.' The weather is still cold. I have to be wearing a lot and a lot.

The street in the 'Jungle' is not just a street; it is a road of life with all its sadness, happiness, hope and disappointments. Anytime I came back from a try, sometimes at dawn, when I walked in this street after maybe five, six or more hours of walking, running and escaping the police in the freezing weather, the first step in this street was like the first step in paradise. Still, I feel the escape in my chest; I have a cough. Heavy steps. I say to myself, 'Just, just one step.' I am so tired and cold; I cough and cough. I can see this street: Finally, 'Have I arrived in the 'Jungle'?', I take a deep breath: 'Yes.' My cold and wet shelter – that is a palace in paradise for me. A real palace.

Babak (from Iran):
I have seen a lot of people trying the most dangerous ways every night. One of my friends from our container, he jumped on the track here and he hid on the track for two days without anything. After two days, he lost hope and went back. They risk their lives going there. They don't know what is waiting them in the UK but every night they are trying in the most dangerous

FIGURE 4.11

This is close to the camp, just before the bridge. It is one of my friends.
I asked him to sleep in the train rail. Photo by Babak (from Iran).

ways. They are walking the long way. Sometimes a
train passes and they try to jump on the track or they
go to another train station. It is two hours' walking. I
worry about them. I have been here for three months
so I know them very well. We are very close, also
because we are living very close in the small container.
We are friends so I will be worried about them if they
go one night and don't come back. Then I call them;
one will be on the track, another on the train station
and maybe one of them made it and passed.

Riaz (from Pakistan):
30 March 2016: There was a traffic jam on the highway
crossing the 'Jungle' today and refugees were trying to
get onto lorries. The police couldn't control it so they

191

threw tear gas towards refugees to discourage them so they would not come and try, but they still tried. Meanwhile, some refugees threw stones towards the police. The police responded with tear gas and rubber bullets and many people's eyes and throats got hurt.

14 October 2016: A refugee died this morning in Loon-Plage. Three migrants who were on the tracks in Loon-Plage got caught by a train at 7am; one dead.

Attempts to get on or under a vehicle are, as reported by Babak and Riaz, dangerous and sometimes fatal. To camp residents, congested traffic on the main road next to the camp can be an opening into such attempts. However, as the French authorities are aware of this tactic, physical and sometimes violent confrontations occur. Muhammad tells in the following about his first attempt to leave together with the Kurdish group he introduced in Chapter 3 – an attempt initiated by a traffic jam and followed by a range of other difficult, violent and dispiriting events:

Muhammad (from Syria):
That night, the Kurdish group wanted to attempt to get to the UK. 'Dogar' means when the traffic is jammed in the port or train station, and the lorries stop, one behind the other over a long distance and for a long time. The refugees can then try to ride the lorries and hide themselves in their trunks or under the lorries, between the wheels on the hub, and sneak to the port in this way.

On the night, when the Kurdish group wanted to attempt to get to the UK, I went with them to the highway. They wanted to cross and block the road to force the lorries to stop; this is called, 'artificial dogar'. It was such a stupid attempt; nothing was organised or prepared. They did not even know the way.

It was midnight, and we walked for more than one-and-a-half hours. It was a very cold night, 5–7 degrees below zero. Everything was completely frozen. The group chose a point on a bridge to block the road. It was far from police cars, about 150–200 metres away. They were not experts at all, so they failed and the police discovered us. We had to run. I did not know the way, but I ran too.

Suddenly, I found myself in a dirty branch of the main river. At first, I didn't know what to do. I sunk in the river up to my head and it was even deeper than that. I swam to the other side, about 3–4 metres, and stayed in the water for some moments until the police went away. I got out of the river. I felt that there was someone holding my hand to help me, but there was no one – it was only my imagination. I was so heavy; my clothes had absorbed the water. It was cold and I was wearing three jackets and three pairs of trousers. I was wet through to my underwear.

I started to run because there was tear gas coming from the police. When I reached a place far from them, I met my friends and started to check my pockets. All the money, my mobile phone, my camera, my tablet and my passport were filled with water.

The guys wanted to try again but I had to go back to the 'Jungle'. I did not know the way, so I went with two other boys who also did not know how to go back. We walked and I was heavy with water. My broken foot started to pain me – a kind of pain that I had never felt. Little by little, my clothes started to freeze and the ice rose on my shoulders and shoes. We were lost and walked for more than two hours for nothing. Later, when we were already exhausted, I discovered that one of the guys who was walking with me had a mobile phone with internet and GPS. He was such a crazy man. I took his phone, saw the location, and in that way, we reached the 'Jungle'. I was angry with him because he did not use his phone when we were lost.

When I arrived back at my room, or shelter, everything was frozen. The jackets I wore were like wood, solid ice. It was difficult to take them off. I changed my clothes, my friends prepared my place to sleep and I slept.

The next day, I realised the situation. My camera, tablet and phone were not working, they were completely damaged, so I lost all my connections. I dried my passport and money. Luckily I had forgotten my papers, my diploma and certificates, when I went to attempt to get to the UK. It took me more than three or four days to dry my clothes on the fire. After this beginning, I knew how hard it would be.

So, my first attempt finished in the river.

After a few days, a new friend called Faisal, from Tell-Hassel, took me on a journey into Calais by bikes. Faisal was the leader of our group, the most experienced man, and a support for all the Syrian Kurd groups, a gentle and respectful man. I'm lucky to know him.

Taking a chance, we tried to sneak to the port and succeeded, but we didn't do anything further that day; we just went back to the 'Jungle'.

The third attempt: me, Faisal and Ahmed were at the same point as the first night I tried. We stood on the highway waiting for the lorries to come, but unfortunately, there were no lorries stopping that day.

After standing there more than one hour on that rainy, windy day, the police discovered us. We crawled on hands and knees to escape the police, but there were too many of them – four or five cars. They arrested us and took us to the police station. We didn't know exactly for what we had been arrested, but clearly, we were trying to reach the port and maybe it was illegal to be at the highway? By the evening, after checking us, they let us go. It was too far to go by foot from the police station to the camp. There was a supermarket, so we went to buy some food. Then we tried to go back to the bridge. I saw a car of gendarmerie. They were looking at us so I went up to them before they thought about coming to us.

'Good evening', I said.

'Good evening', they replied.

'We are lost here, and I want to ask you the way, please', and I bent a little forward and placed my hands on the glass of the door of the car.

'Where do you want to go?' the police officer asked.

'To the "Jungle"', I replied.

'Are you from the "Jungle"?'

'Yes.'

When I said that, he changed the tone of his voice and the look on his face and shouted, 'Take your hand from the car!'

I did that, and asked him again about the way. He said something, and gestured with his hand. Frankly,

I did not understand, but I said, 'Thank you', and left. We took a bus to go back to the 'Jungle'.

After a few days, I went with Mustafa and Ahmed to see the train station. We expected that there would be a 'dogar', so we left in the morning. It was rainy, windy and cold. The police stopped us, but we escaped. Later, the gendarmerie saw us, ordered us to go back to the 'Jungle' and followed us for a while to make sure.

Again, like the previous day, we changed our destination and went back towards the station. There is a park near a castle in the area. We went to wait there and observe the situation. Later, so many people from the 'Jungle' arrived, the police came again and asked us to leave the park. This time, they bombed us with tear gas. One of them was shouting in French. I did not understand his words. He was pointing the gun at me; he was about 4 metres away. Although I told him, 'Calm down, I'm leaving', he shot. Unfortunately, the tear gas canister exploded. By luck, it was next to me, not on my face. We hid ourselves for a while and later I realised that we should go back. It was nearly sunset, and it was dangerous to walk in Calais in the night; many people had been beaten up there.

Every other night, me, Ahmed and Mustafa and another kind boy, Elias, were trying to reach the port by way of the beach. Taking advantage of the tide, we took much time to sneak there, and usually we failed. It was hard to walk or run on the wet sand. Yes, our night operations were as you would see it in Hollywood movies. One time, I remember, the policemen were standing just above our heads on a sand dune, but in the end, we escaped.

All our attempts failed. God was telling me, 'It is not your place, you are not here for this reason.' Twenty days passed in which so many events happened and I saw so many things. I'll tell you about some of them now.

On the third day after I reached the 'Jungle', at 1.00am, someone knocked on my door and a voice said, 'Doctor, please hurry up, we need you.' I hurried to see what was wrong. There were three guys, two from Kobanî and their friend Faisal from Tell Tamer. They were completely covered with blood and nearly unconscious. Their cases were as follows. One of them had a wound on his upper lip, was complaining of pain in his spine, couldn't stand and had trauma to his chest and legs. One had two wounds on his scalp, about 5cm, and a fracture in his skull in the occipital area. The third had a fracture in his face, the left zygomatic bone, a wound in his scalp and trauma to his left arm. Their faces were pale and yellowish in colour. This was my first impression and I told them that they needed hospitalisation. We called the ambulance, but it didn't come. A woman called Hannah, and a Belgian man helped us with their car to rescue those injured persons and take them to Calais hospital.

As soon as we got to the hospital, I entered the emergency room and asked for help: 'Please, I have three injured persons in a bad situation who need help.' Nothing happened – no one moved. The Belgian man, who knew French, asked again but still nothing happened. We carried the boys into the emergency room using wheelchairs. After that, the hospital staff did nothing for more than one hour. The guys were in shock and feeling a lot of pain. Technically, I don't believe that the people who were in the hospital that night were doctors. I don't know exactly whether they were doctors or not. They looked like they didn't know what they were doing. I never saw doctors like them before – so slow, so cold, so stupid – irresponsible. No one spoke English in the hospital; it was difficult to communicate with them.

After I explained the cases for them, they took about four hours to suture three wounds. After three hours or more, they did some blood tests and gave some intravenous fluids with an analgesic. After I insisted, they took them for X-rays: it was about 7 in the morning. I was so angry to see ignorance and irresponsibility like this in a hospital.

At the hospital, I saw two other injured children, no more than 15 years old. They were attacked on the same night, also in Calais. All the injured had been attacked in the city by an unknown group with metal bars after being robbed of their money and possessions. No one knew the group but the police were not beyond suspicion, as many people were suggesting that the group were police or some fascists related to the police.

After those Kurdish guys were attacked, there was a demonstration in Calais to support the refugees and to demand the UK to open its borders for refugees like all other countries. We made our mark on this demonstration; Ahmed and I designed a banner and carried it.

A few days after, while it was raining in the afternoon, a voice came from outside saying, 'Dogar dogar.'

There were many lorries stuck on the road near the port entrance, but the road is protected by fences with barbed wire. People would need to cut the fence and the barbed wire to go through. Too many police were controlling the road and there were a lot of people from the 'Jungle' coming to have a 'chance'. Our Kurdish group was one of the first, and so the battle started. Some groups were hitting police cars with stones to let others have time to cut the fence. The police bombed us with a huge amount of tear gas and pepper spray. The conflicts continued for more than two hours. Eventually, we gave up and went back to our 'Jungle'. We were tired.

By the time my period of attempts to reach the UK ended, the British government had accepted four Syrian children to travel to UK legally. Then a Syrian, who had been in the 'Jungle' for six to seven months, made a list of all the Syrian names in the 'Jungle'. We didn't know why, but people said that the lawyers would study the probability of allowing Syrians to go to the UK. They said that a decision would be reached after the 22nd of February so my friends decided to wait for that date. I waited with them for another ten days and that's what made me go to school in 'Jungle Books Library', because I had free time.

Soon, things started to get more and more complicated. There was a lawsuit against the 'Jungle' by the government; the court was in Lille. Because of that, for the last week of my life in the 'Jungle', there was a meeting every night for volunteers, and other 'Jungle' people, discussing this issue, planning for all options and preparing themselves for any developments.

For me, and from the beginning, I expected that the government would follow its own decision, and that they were just wasting time to absorb the reactions. I was thinking, while attending the meetings, that only a few of those attending would be present when any conflict arose between the refugees and the government.

On the day of the court judgment, the judge came to have a look at the 'Jungle' before giving her last verdict on this issue in Lille. All volunteers, media journalists, agencies and so on were in the 'Jungle' in the morning at 8.00am, and woke all the people up to show the judge how many people – families, children and youth – were actually living in the 'Jungle'. If there was to be an eviction, these human beings would lose their places and remain in these bad circumstances, homeless, without care.

The court was meeting at 2.00pm. At 11.30am, I went to Lille with Faisal and Hannah, in her car with two other people, but we were not allowed to enter the court hall. The judge didn't give her final verdict, which made people optimistic thinking they had a big chance to win the case. It was the opposite for me. If the judge had wanted to decide in our favour, she would not have been shy to give her verdict immediately. I thought that this was again a plan to absorb the reaction by delaying the verdict. In this way, little by little, the media and even the people would be bored by the time of the final verdict. They would feel that they were waiting there for nothing and just wasting time.

The decision to proceed, when the court finally gave its decision agreeing to destroy part of the 'Jungle', came to light after three to four days. The government didn't apply the court decision immediately. They waited for another three days and started on Monday 29 February 2016, the day when I left the 'Jungle'. I think this delay was, again, to avoid the reactions and the presence of the media.

In this period, Faisal had made his last attempt to get to the UK from Belgium and had been arrested there by the government. He arrived back at 5am in a very bad state after a terrible journey. Fouad and Elias were attempting to cross from another city, Dunkirk, every other day, with the aid of an Iraqi Kurdish smuggler, but they didn't succeed. Nothing came from the British government about the Syrians, and on the other side, the French government was controlling everything severely. It was controlling and monitoring every way and place that people might try to sneak through to the port or train station.

In the same period, I went with Pedro and some other guys to film some videos outside of the 'Jungle' for his documentary film. Unknowingly, he took us to a ferry controlled by some smugglers that attacked us in the car. The event could have been very dangerous if they had succeeded in stopping our car. These days, if you want to go to the UK using smugglers, you have to pay from £5000 to £10,000. A few smugglers control each region of the coast and don't allow anyone to step inside their region without paying.

When it seemed impossible to go to the UK, I turned towards my friends and said, 'Now all of you have to leave with me. It is time to leave the UK behind and start to think seriously in our lives, so

all of you have to go with me to another country –
Germany.' That was what I said, and we decided to
leave on Monday 29 February 2016.

I will not go to the country that just wants rich men
who can pay for smugglers. I'll not go to a country
whose government talks all the time about human
rights and helping refugees but closes their borders
against them; a government that does everything to
keep the refugees away from their borders, far from
their land – those people who are escaping death, ignorance and poverty, and dictatorships supported by
western countries.

Shaheen, part of whose story of persecution by the Taliban
in Afghanistan, and of his long and torturous journey to and
through Europe, we have already heard, came quickly from
Paris to Calais. Here, his attempts to reach the UK started
almost immediately; however, because of an injury acquired
during one of these attempts, Shaheen, like Muhammad,
ended up changing his plans:

Shaheen (from Afghanistan):
After eight hours, we reached Paris. We got down
from the bus and looked for someone to guide us on
how we could go to the Calais 'Jungle'. We found a
man who knew English and he helped us. At last we
reached the Calais 'Jungle'. That time was very strange
for us and the weather was very cold, so I found a volunteer worker and asked for a tent. Thanks to him, we
received a blanket and a tent. I was very tired and I
slept. When I woke up in the morning, I saw a new
world: a lot of people from different countries, a lot

of volunteers; they were helping people. To be honest, I liked it, so I spent all day walking about. At last I found a guy and asked him, 'How can I go to the UK?' He said, 'It's very hard to do.' Then he explained everything to me and he said, 'There is an agent, you have to talk with him.' So I talked with the agent. He said, 'You have to pay €500, then I will make a game for you.' I told him that 'I don't have that much money.' So he said, 'How much can you pay?' I said, 'Only two hundred.' Then he said, 'Ok.' He said, 'Be ready for the night, we are going to close the autobahn, and then my man will break the locks of the container and will get you onto the container so you can hide there. There are two police check posts: one is the French police and the other one is Britain's police check post. When you have crossed these two check posts then the container will go into the ship. After some hours, you will be in England.' I was happy: 'That's very easy.'

At night, the agents closed the road and made some fires on the road. They stopped the containers. We were among some guys waiting for them to open the doors of the containers so we could climb up into them. At last, they broke down the locks of some containers and they shouted to us, 'Get in the containers!' We got in and hid under the cartons, and they locked the door from outside. Then the container moved towards the UK. At the first check post of the French police, there were dogs with the police who found us, arrested us and kept us for the whole night. Then they took us to the police station where they wrote our names down and released us and we went back to the

'Jungle'. We slept the whole day and in the evening, the agents made a group and again they were trying to put us in a moving container. They broke down the locks of the container and some guys climbed onto them. Suddenly, when I was climbing, I fell down from the container and I broke the last part of my backbone (the coccyx). That was very painful for me. I couldn't even walk because of the pain. Some guys took me back to the 'Jungle'. I didn't sleep all night because of the pain. At last, in the morning, I went to the doctors and explained what had happened. They gave me painkiller tablets, took me to the hospital, and took some X rays. Then they told me, 'You have broken your coccyx and we have to do an operation.' I was shaken up: 'What sort of operation? Is it something serious?' They said, 'Yes, we have to do the operation.' I said, 'No, I don't want to have an operation!' I insisted so much, 'I don't want to do it.' I told the doctors, 'Give me some medicines.' They told me, 'Don't waste your time; after some weeks, you won't be able to do the operation, then it will be too late for you.' I told them, 'Give me the medicines, and after some time I will decide.'

They gave me some medicines and I started taking them. I felt well for some time. But after some months, the weather became cloudy and it started raining, and we had no beds at that time – we were sleeping on the ground – and that was not good for me because of my injury. Then I went again to the doctor who checked everything. He said, 'Now it's very late for an operation.' I said, 'Why? I want to do it now.' He said,

'You can't do it now, it's too late.' Then I said, 'What should I do now?' He said, 'You have to take care of yourself. You will suffer this pain for a long time, probably for your whole life.' He was right. Still now, I have pain and I can't even sit on a hard chair, the ground, or something else very hard.

With a very broken heart, I came back to my tent and I cried so much. I said to myself, 'I will never retreat; I will go to UK, and that's my dream.' Then I rested for some time and again I started trying to cross the border, but I couldn't succeed. At last I decided, 'I am going to save my life. Whether it is the UK or France, they are the same for me.' Then I went to the people of OFPRA in the 'Jungle' and told them, 'I want to claim asylum in France.' They became very happy and wrote my name down and told me, 'Tomorrow we will take you to the asylum centre.' They took me to the asylum seekers' centre, where they explained everything to me.

Leaving

Despite the many challenges of living in the 'Jungle', its communities and living spaces, especially for those staying over longer periods, come to represent new homes that are left behind when moving on to a new uncertain situation. As we have now heard, some gave up on the idea of reaching the UK, at least for the time being. Instead, they focused on other countries or applied for asylum in France. Here Muhammad, who decided to leave for Germany, tells about his last day in the 'Jungle':

Muhammad (from Syria):

Saying goodbye to the camp is like leaving your home once more. It includes separation from people to whom there has been established close connections. I went to have my last look at everything. It all looked meaningless and sad. The streets were empty; my heart was beating quickly. Every time I looked at the 'Jungle' shelters, tents, restaurants, refugees, volunteers … everything, everything was attracting me and bringing strange feelings. I had become linked to this place. I felt as if I was leaving my real home.

I went to the library to have a last look in the afternoon. There was my teacher, giving a French lesson to some students in the conversation room. I stopped for a little, and stood not far away, listening. I was smiling, but inside me there was something like a gap of missing memories. I took a book from the library and left without saying goodbye.

When I was in the bus, I realised that this is really the end. So many things are left behind. So many friends. So many attempts and too many wishes and too much love. An unknown future is waiting.

Everything that has a beginning has an end. Those were the last words running through my mind the night before I left the 'Jungle'. They were telling me, 'You know that goodbye is painful, but this should end. You must not stay like this forever.' The voice was telling me, 'Your job here is done, another job is waiting somewhere else. There are people who want you and who need you there too. For this journey, it is enough; this operation has reached its end.' I remembered my last day when I left Kobanî, before the war. My last day when I left the hospital in Aleppo. My last day when I left my home in Syria. My last day and last day and ... and now, my last day in the 'Jungle'. Always, the same feelings come. They cannot be expressed in words. Calais was for me like a school. I think I deserve a graduation. My life here gave me new views and visions and ways.

Eritrea (from Eritrea):
When I reached Calais, I asked the people I knew there how to get to England. They told me to go to the train station where they would show me how they attempt to get to England. I went there with them one day. I was tired. 'Oh my God, what should I do?' I went through so many challenges and now I am facing another one. I asked people why they did not seek asylum in France. A guy told me that he applied, he didn't get accepted and he waited for four months where they didn't give him any shelter. 'You have to go to the UK', he said.

I stayed in Calais for one month. After one month, I won. I checked the weather forecast on my phone and it said that there would be a heavy rain the next day. I used the rain to win. I went to the train station with two others and we got on top of the train. There were many cars on the train and we were under the cars. Even if they had looked for us, they would not have found us because of the heavy rain. A security man saw us and brought a dog, but the dog was afraid of the rain. Thank you God for sending the rain. When

I entered the tunnel I shouted and no one could hear me. I shouted because I was very happy: 'I am going to England!!', 'Thank God!!'

We will end this chapter with a poem written by Babak. Altogether, living in and leaving the 'Jungle' constitutes one of the many 'wars' that 'Jungle' residents have gone through and will keep on fighting. Babak writes about a hopefulness that remains despite the challenges. This will lead us to the next chapter about life after the 'Jungle', the futures that the authors face and the dreams they have for their future lives.

Babak (from Iran):
I'm walking on a path, rubble under my feet, pieces of wood under my feet, on the right side high fences, high walls and closed doors, on the left side green nature, beautiful views and endless gardens.

I just walk, I don't mind the rubble.

I enjoy walking on the pieces of wood, I don't mind about the fences, I enjoy the green gardens.

I don't cut the fences, I don't knock on the closed doors, I just pass through them, I shoot my tiredness with the rubble.

Some thoughts are fighting in my head, like a war of devils vs angels, like a war of my fists vs walls, like a war of my hands vs the cold weather, like a war of me and nostalgia, like a war of me and the French language, like a war of me and strange looks, like a war of my eyes and police eyes, like a war of hands vs fences, like a war of nation vs government, like a war of birds and borders.

After all of these wars, my eyes are looking at a rabbit behind the fences, like he is in prison, and he also looks the same way on me! Truly, who's the prisoner? Me or him?

Who knows what's at the end of this way?

Who knows how tired my legs are?

Who knows in this cold and dark 'Jungle' how a warm heart beats?

Who knows how many dreams will be killed in my head at midnight?

And who knows with which dream I will wake up?

Who knows what's going on between me and my friends in these containers?

Who knows with a beautiful rain how many people will be cold?

Who knows how many eyes will cry at midnight?

I forget all of the bad thoughts by looking at a flower, I laugh and walk on the pieces of wood, like me playing in my childhood. It seems I won all these wars and I found all the answers!

And at the end of this one-way road on which you can never go back, after all of these green and dark ways, maybe at the last station, where the sky and rail kiss each other, my mother will wait for me with a beautiful flower, my father will invite me for a hot tea and my brother will play with me like childhood in our yard.

So until my mother's flower is waiting for me,

While my father's tea is still hot and my brother's game is not finished,

I Will Walk

CHAPTER 5

Life after the 'Jungle'

Introduction

This chapter tells the story of some of the authors after they left the 'Jungle', and looks at their future aspirations. Some authors were still living in the camp when they discussed what they would do once they had the opportunity to leave the place, whereas others had already left the camp. Some reached the UK, whereas a few continued their journey to another country in Europe. Others chose to claim asylum in France and were either taken to a new shelter in another part of the country, often in a remote area, or stayed close to the Calais camp, with the support of local charities or local citizens. Those who left the 'Jungle' often expressed mixed feelings about their time in the camp. Some authors are still very attached to the place and the people they met there. Others have put this experience behind them to concentrate on their new life.

Leaving the 'Jungle' for good: First moments away

Mani, an artist from Iran, left the 'Jungle' a few months ago. He remembered the trip:

Mani (from Iran):

We were in the truck, a fridge container, for more than 16 hours. On that last night, when our trafficker put me in the lorry with 15 other people, I had no idea that this time would be the time that I was successful. I just thought to myself that this try would be like all of the other times that I had tried to make the crossing.

As I was searching for a good corner of the lorry to hide in, I thought to myself, 'I wonder which way we will go this time? Which city of France? Belgium perhaps? The Netherlands? Italy? Spain? Or maybe Russia? If this lorry goes to Russia, how many days will I have to walk to get back to Calais?' All of these thoughts were going through my head.

The lorry was full of boxes of German beer. Where would they end up? Who would drink them? There was complete darkness and silence inside the coldness of the refrigerated truck. We could hear voices from outside. 'Where are we?' I whispered. 'We are inside the ferry,' my Afghan friend whispered back to me. 'I don't think so, we can't be,' I replied, not daring to believe it to be true. We tried to guess where we were by listening to the voices going on around us outside the truck, the voices of women. We could hear the voice of one woman making announcements but we couldn't understand what she was saying. And then the lorry stopped.

Where could we be? On the ferry? At a Belgian train station? Where?

After about an hour, the lorry started up again and we felt it move at high speed. It felt as though we were on a motorway.

I started to worry that the lorry was going to Belgium. How was I going to get back to the 'Jungle' with no money and no documents? Someone from inside the lorry said, 'No, the lorry is in the UK!' I couldn't believe it, I didn't want to let myself believe it. I had tried time and time again, more than 20 times, to make the crossing. Each time we were found by police, each time was the wrong place, the wrong time, the wrong everything and each time I had to make my way back to the 'Jungle'. It was not easy and with each failure it became more and more difficult.

My Afghan friend then showed me his mobile phone. The time on his phone had gone back one hour to UK time. Then I could let myself believe that it was true, we were in the UK.

When we were all sure that we were in the UK and that we were far enough away from the border to be safe, we started to celebrate and shout with joy. We were all very thirsty and we had a truck full of the best German beer.

After three hours, we were tired and a little bit tipsy; we needed to get out. We started to shout and knock on the walls of the truck to try and get the attention of the driver but he couldn't hear us and just carried on.

Our elation turned to sadness, our joy to worry. We had a new problem now. Because of our frolics and celebrations we had used up what oxygen there was in the truck and we were all struggling to breathe. We had finally made it to the UK but were we all now going to die in the container? Was that to be our destiny? Was this really where life was going to end? What a stupid fate!

Eventually the lorry stopped and, after about half an hour, the police opened the doors of the truck.

FIGURE 5.1

'To UK or not UK' – Mani arrived in the UK on the 400th anniversary of
Shakespeare's death. When coming into the UK, a picture of Shakespeare was
one of the first things he saw. Cartoons by Mani (from Iran).

Eritrea and Refugees' Voice also explained their first encounters with the British police after they each made it to the UK. Despite their very different histories, both then had to wait for their claims to be decided:

Eritrea (from Eritrea):
I was on the train until it reached its destination. Then the security people came, and I was laughing because I was happy. I did not consider whether they were going to detain me or not, it was not on my mind.

People in Calais did advise me regarding what to tell the police and about specific tricks. I didn't accept it. I was thinking that I must tell the truth. I spoke the truth and I am still waiting for my interview.

I registered with the police and they told me that they would detain me, but fortunately, it was only for one night. They asked me screening questions and I answered the truth. They brought me to what we call the Britannia Hotel, and after that they took me to Liverpool and from there to here, this town in the north of England.

Now I am living here, I know you and I know many English people. They are very nice people. Although it is difficult, it is better than the challenges I have been through. They give us £5 per day. I can't say it is a good amount of money, but it is their rule and I don't have any comments about this because I don't have the knowledge. It is not too much but we use that money and we are living.

Refugees' Voice (from Afghanistan):
When I came back to the UK, they caught me and

they asked me, 'Do you want to claim asylum?' And I said, 'No.' So they said, 'We are going to send you back.' So I told them that I had claimed asylum back in the year 2000 and I gave them my refugee reference number and I gave them all my details. And they checked and asked me. 'This is you?' And I said, 'Yes it is.' And then they asked me if I had a place to live or if I needed accommodation and I told them I had an accommodation. And they released me the same day. They kept me for maybe, seven to eight hours. So I came here to London. I started to live in one friend's place, then another friend. My case is still pending and therefore they could not deport me. But this time I am trying to make things work. I hope that in three months they will give a decision and hopefully it will be a positive. There is a possibility that it will be a negative. I want to go to university but I can't because I haven't got documents.

Others had to abandon the idea of going to the UK. Shaheen, as we heard in the previous chapter, became injured trying to get to the UK, and decided to claim asylum in France. As for others, this was not a straightforward process:

Shaheen (from Afghanistan)
So at last, I decided to stay in France. I wrote my name down for a city in France for asylum. After some days, they took me to a city by the name of La-Seyne-Sur-Mer, and that was a very good city, I liked it. After several days, they took me to the OFPRA centre for fingerprints, and they took my prints. Thanks to God, there are none of my fingerprints in any other

European countries. So they gave me the right for asylum in France. Our social worker, a woman, wrote all of my story, with all the evidence of it which I have, and I sent it to OFPRA in Paris.

Then I asked my social worker for a French course. She promised me the class, but it took two months. I was asking her every day in order to make her find a French class for me. I was very happy that day, because I have a strong interest in learning the French language. So I started the French class and attended it for two months.

After those two months, they shifted me from that city to another city, by the name of La Verpellière. Now I am living in La Verpellière; there are no courses, no activities to do, and still I am waiting for my interview. In Calais, when OFPRA was first talking to me, they told me, 'Your whole process will be finished in maximum, three months', but it's seven months, and I am still waiting just for my interview.

You know, every day, I am making a new promise to my little daughter, 'I will take you to France, I will take you to France', and now she is not talking with me. I asked my wife, 'Why is she is not talking with me?' Her mother said, 'She is saying, "Dad is lying to me, I don't want to talk with him"', and that's very panicking for me. But this pain, anyone who has a daughter, knows. So let's hope for better. But a refugee's life is like that; you have to spend a lot of life in waiting.

Muhammad also gave up his hopes of going to the UK, after he had tried many times, over the course of a month, to cross. After then, he went to Germany to join other family members, as he had planned:

Muhammad (from Syria):
I left with Abdul firstly; the others would catch up with us later. After leaving Calais, we went to Paris with our heavy luggage. We didn't know where to go because we had to wait in Paris from 12.00am to 10.40pm for the next journey to Germany. Luckily, Abdul found an Arabian restaurant and called a French friend, Sonia, living in Paris. When she came, and after eating lunch, we left our suitcases in the restaurant and started a journey around Paris. Sonia was a gift from heaven that day, because we were sad and tired and nearly hopeless, but after she came, everything turned around to be better. She was our tourist guide; walking, we visited many historical places. It was a very nice day in Paris that I'll never forget. I was so happy and excited, enjoying my time, forgetting for a moment the 'Jungle' and its sorrows, and all the memories we left behind. My feet started to hurt and pain me, because of my shoes. They were not good, and they harmed my feet, which became swollen, painful and hot. In spite of that, I continued walking. We walked more than four hours, and saw many historical places in Paris. It was a very nice journey, so I hid my pain till the night, when I took off my shoes to see how bad my feet had become.

At 10.48pm we started the last stage of our journey to Germany. I had a notebook I was using to write my French lessons, and at the same time I wrote there all of my friends' emails, phone numbers and addresses.

Unfortunately, I forgot that notebook, along with my gloves, in the bus, and now all my friends' emails and numbers from the 'Jungle' are lost forever. Maybe it was a message to leave 'Jungle' life behind and start a new life, because a part of me was in the 'Jungle'; or maybe it is destiny that will choose just the friends who really care for me – they will find me if they look for me. I was still related to the 'Jungle', as if a part of my soul was still there. It was only a month but it felt as much as a year; it was really one year of work and evidence and experience. And it was also not long at all; I didn't feel at the time that the days were passing.

When I began my journey from Diyarbakir, I said, 'The operation starts.' At about 6 a.m. on Tuesday I arrived at my brother's home in Germany and took to the PC to say, 'The operation has ended, but the mission is not completed yet.'

In describing his goodbyes to the 'Jungle', Muhammad wrote, 'As I see it, Calais and the "Jungle" are not parts of France or even Europe.' His postscript to his leaving shows that, despite being happy to reunite with family members in Germany, he felt he had left a part of his new Calais family behind him:

Muhammad (from Syria):
It has now been more than a week since I finished my last journey. Still I have something inside me; I don't know what kind of feeling it is. It is not the first time. It is a kind of sad feeling about something that you left behind. You lost it, and will never see or have it again forever. I'm back with my family, with my old

friends. That temporary life and those feelings just came to you and left as a dream, leaving their effect on you. It seems that humans will always go back to their origins, their old ways, so they shouldn't be tied to temporary life and relations. It will all go and leave you heartbroken; only a few memories will remain. Overall, we all belong to our origin, and only that origin will welcome us again and again, so don't forget your homelands, your family and nice memories. Care for them and make them happy and the best, as much as you can. Be grateful that you have them and know that any other thing could be fake and will disappear one day. You will return to your origin and only it will give you its warm cuddles. All my family and friends: maybe I was absent from you for a while, for an aim, but I never forgot you.

Similarly, Refugees' Voice wrote, after reaching the UK:

Refugees' Voice (from Afghanistan):
The time I was in Calais was better than now to be honest, mentally, and in my heart I was in peace. Now I am struggling and working hard trying to get my life on track again; it made me realise things, that I needed to solve things for myself. So Calais made me realise that. In a way I do miss Calais. I was happier there, even though I was living in very tough conditions; my activities were good. Currently, I see all the things that are going on and it makes me feel kind of upset. I miss that place, it was like 'helping everybody'; I was happy there and with all my activities and now I am struggling and I am fighting for myself.

After leaving: A new uncertain journey

Most camp residents' views of French people were strongly affected by the French riot police surrounding the camp and local people's hostility and violence, reinforcing the refugees' aspirations to go to the UK. French government accommodation centres (*Centres d'Accueil et d'Orientation*) were often in remote places with limited facilities, providing very small food grants; rooms may be shared between people, at times from warring national groups. For those who chose to live outside CAOs, life could be very hard as they had to rely on other kinds of support such as those provided by family, as in the case of Zeeshan Javid and Zeeshan Imayat who moved to Paris to stay with a cousin. Moreover, many camp residents who applied for asylum in France expressed the fear of being returned to the country they first reached when entering the EU, or of being deported from France after a failed asylum application, causing high anxiety, as for Milkesa:

> *Milkesa (from Ethiopia):*
> In keeping with their country's respected human-itarian tradition, laws and regulation, norms and international obligations, I submitted my asylum appeal to the relevant department of the French government. I escaped ethnic persecution and severe human rights abuse in Ethiopia. I can't return to Ethiopia to restructure my life due to the political accusations against me. There is no justice in Ethiopia. There is no resource that will ensure my civil rights. So I fear I will face the worst fate and get killed. I left

the 'Jungle' to ask for asylum in France; just for my safety, freedom and human dignity – thinking to visit the UK at some point in the future. I think my future is uncertain, wherever I am.

My hope and ambition to write about the situation that I have been experiencing in the southern French city where I am living is great. But my asylum process with the Court is under question, as France is rejecting almost all refugees. One month from the date you receive the court decision, if it is a negative decision, the government forces you to leave your house; and then you sleep on the streets. Everything will be cut from you, such as medical and food assistance, and money allowance; they issue no more valid documents. And then forced deportation follows. I signed my asylum application, this document, and its copy is in my hand now. What this means, is that I am always thinking and worrying about my possible forced deportation, under French law, tomorrow or any day. Forced deportation is every minute's major and minor possibility for me. Hence I can't write anything more yet, and I don't think I will write anything, before I am issued with the document that allows me to stay in France. Otherwise, I am thinking about when I will be thrown into the streets and get forced deportation.

Thank God, I escaped from the jaws of the Ethiopian government – I am out of the fire now. But if deportation is awaiting me at some point in the future, my current living has no meaning. Sleeping on the streets of France is not better or safer than my Ethiopian house. I can't see any hope of a bright future. I am in a turbulent situation and times of turmoil.

Among those who made it to the UK, absence of social and emotional support characterised their first months – often a huge change from the support they were used to receiving in the camp from other refugees, volunteers and grassroots organisations:

Africa (from Sudan):
I have had my initial screening interview. I do not have much contact with my lawyer; she just tells me I must wait. I am not allowed to work. I cannot volunteer formally unless a volunteer organisation writes a letter to the Home Office for me, to ask for permission. I do not want to do this; the Home Office might not like it. Waiting and doing nothing is hard – I like to be busy and to organise things. Sometimes I wish I was in the 'Jungle', my 'shining city'. Conditions were very difficult, but I could do many things. I volunteer informally near where I live; I worked for a charity providing clothes for refugees for a month, for a church that provides food, and now I am translating for new Syrian families who come here and do not know any English. I am hoping to take some English classes, but the college will ring me later; the classes are full at the moment. There are some martial arts classes that will also start up again soon.

Before, I was living with people who did not speak English or Arabic. It was very isolating. Now, I am living with one person from Sudan. He has received only £19 from the Home Office since he arrived over two months ago. I think there has been a managerial error. I have rung the Home Office for him but so far no money has arrived. I am buying him food from my money and we are cooking together. £35 a week is not much for two people. But I cannot let him starve.

You can feel racism sometimes in people's eyes when they look at you, and in the expressions on their faces. Usually, I ignore it, or I pretend I didn't see it. It is less in London, because there are people from many different places there, unlike here in this small Welsh city.

When I am in the city centre, I take tea in a café run by Eritreans. Many Africans go there. I feel relaxed, because I do not experience racism there. Yesterday, I had a bus ticket to go home from the city centre. The bus driver asked me where I wanted to go, and then he said that the bus did not go there, even though I knew it was the right bus. I told him that it was not his business where I was going, or why. But I got off the bus, and I caught the next one.

Sometimes I have trouble sleeping, and bad dreams. The doctor gave me some sleeping pills, but I only took a few; I do not want to get addicted. The Home Office does not treat us as people; they do not want to see or hear us. They treat us worse than they might treat an animal.

Syrian refugees get help quickly. But their situation is not worse than that of many other people. I think the UK feels guilty that it has not helped Syria. But it is not good to create inequalities between people. We are all escaping war or persecution; why make differences between us? You can't feel the same as a refugee, I think. You can imagine, and give a little support, but it is not much. Refugees have lost a lot. Even when they get their status, they are not in the same place as they were before. Of course, some people are stronger than others. But I think that all refugees have lost some of their original personalities .... .

The British racism and xenophobia described above also appeared in Mani's account of an early meeting with a man who was drunk and homeless:

Mani (from Iran):
    The night before the EU referendum, I was feeling frustrated, because all of the day, I was unemployed and alone at home. It was about 11.00pm. I went out just for a stroll around the town. In the centre, amidst the sound of loud music, I walked and envied the happy people in the night clubs.
    Suddenly a drunk, poor man came to me.
    He asked me, 'Please help me.'
    I told him, 'I am an asylum seeker, I can't help you.'
    He asked a question, 'You have a home?'
    Me: 'Yes.'
    He: 'Who gave it to you?'
    Me: 'I think it's from the UK government.'
    He: 'I am British and all my life I have been living in this country, but now I haven't a home.'
    I didn't know how I could answer him.
    I was silent and I left him.
    He drank another sip from the bottle he had in his hand.
    And shouted to his homeless friends on the other side of the road,
    'He is a foreigner and the government gave him a house.
    I couldn't understand what they said; maybe they

FIGURE 5.2
The drunk man. Drawing by Mani (from Iran).

were sour to me and the Government.

I preferred to leave them fast, without any answer.

But all the way home, I thought to myself, 'Is their situation because of me?'

All that the asylum seekers wish is to have work permission. We don't want houses, money ... we just want to be a citizen like him. I don't think if we leave he will have a better situation; maybe he will have more money for more drinking.

Full of hope

Work and family aspirations

Majid's 'tries' with what he called an 'an expert smuggler' – that is, one who had a long-term business rather than someone doing it once to make some quick money, or abscond with it – worked out: he reached the UK. Majid's work history gave him confidence for his future in the UK, and he also had plans for seeing his family:

Majid (from Iran):
After you reach the UK, there are two possibilities. If the police catch you, they will send you anywhere. Otherwise, if the police do not catch you, you can spend some time elsewhere before claiming asylum – and then the police and Home Office will disperse you afterwards. All of my family is in Iran. I just have friends in the UK. I graduated in software engineering so I could do this in the UK. I had a business in Iran. But for me, finding a job and working in the UK is not a matter of concern. At the beginning, I would do anything, even labouring jobs.

The conditions of the refugees like me and my Iranian friends vary. We have to stay in the country to which we have gone for asylum for many years. Most of us can't actually go back to our home country. It depends directly on each one's situation and problem.

FIGURE 5.3
Bulldozer (after the first eviction, in March 2016).
Photo by Habibi (from Afghanistan).

For some guys who had political problems, they can never go back until the regime changes. For other guys, with less important reasons – some social problems, or changing their religion – it's possible to go back, but they should wait, get citizenship elsewhere and go to their country with a new passport. I've talked with some guys with UK passports who've lived there many years and all of them said they had no problem going to Iran with their British passport. The Iranian officials ask lots of questions, but after that, it's no problem. They can see their family and friends. It's risky to visit – but I am sure the regime will change in less than ten years, unless they change themselves and respect people more. With my British passport, I am sure I will be able to go to Iran.

I know that you are concerned about me not seeing

my family and friends for maybe ten years – but Iranians have found a solution to this difficulty. They invite their family and friends to Turkey, Malaysia, or Dubai. The only countries you can't go to from Iran are the US, UK and Israel. (Have you seen an Iranian passport? On it is written, 'You can in no circumstances go to Israel.') This is why, even going back with the British passport to Iran, they will ask me lots of questions, as if I am a spy. With a French passport, no problems.

Personally, for me, I can make a new life in the UK. I have some friends there. They told me lots of things about the UK and life conditions. We have different kinds of Iranian communities in the UK: I can be a part of them. As a result, I can build a new life and be successful there. The British government behaves well to Iranians. This situation is not like that in France. From the beginning, when you reach the UK, there is no deportation for Iranians. And they mostly accept Iranians' asylum claims. Iranians are successful in the UK and are respected there; they don't seem to have problems. Most people want to go to London. But for me, it makes no difference, though a larger city is better than somewhere isolated.

Some authors' plans involved work in fields they had not yet been able to enter, as with Habibi, whose family concerns could be met by supportive relatives already in the UK:

Habibi (from Afghanistan):
I came to the 'Jungle' because I wanted to go to England. It would be a good place for me. Especially

the villages, I prefer them over cities. Villages are quiet peaceful places with lovely people, very lovely people. You will be more likely to find such people in villages than in cities – honest people. I would love to go to England. If I go there, I will spend the rest of my life in a village. I will find someone and spend the rest of my life with her, start a new life, new hopes, new dreams. I would love to go there and start working as a photographer and to be a zoologist. I want to study animals. This is one of my dreams. I love animals. In Afghanistan I always watched the Discovery Channel and other animal programmes.

Educational aspirations

Many of the refugees in the 'Jungle' had already pursued their education and had developed a wide range of skills in their countries of origin before reaching Calais. However, all the authors were keen to pursue more education after leaving the camp. Teddy, a nurse, wanted to do more university education:

> *Teddy (from Eritrea):*
> I would like to improve my understanding through education. I appreciate heroes like Nelson Mandela and Malcolm X; I get some support from their strength. I don't want to support anyone blindly though; I want to improve things. You have to judge if an idea is useful for the people. I am interested in courses like civics; I took this after school. I would like to learn more. I don't care about money; I want to improve. I would like to become a full man.

Ali Bajdar had not yet been to university but was committed to getting there; among his other concerns were having a family and helping people, and even though his poor health was a primary concern:

> *Ali Bajdar (from Iraq):*
> My dream is to live just like other people. I don't want there to be war. My dream is to go to school like everyone else. I want a family. A small family, no more than three children. Maybe one or two. I would love to become an accountant. That is because my family never had money so I want to help the poor. My biggest dream (if I had a lot of money) would be to open my own hospital where people could have for instance kidney transplants. I would like to live in the UK because of the health care system, and because my mum said that they can take care of me there. I want to learn English and I was practicing every day in Calais, in the 'Jungle'. I had a good teacher. She said to me that I should not try to jump on a train. It's too dangerous for me. So I don't do that. My friend was trying to jump one night and the guy he was with fell on the tracks.

At the same time, the past remained powerful in his picture of the future:

> My village as I knew it is gone. I don't have my family there. It is all gone. My friend has relatives that drowned in the Aegean Sea. We have lost a lot and every day there is a war going on in Iraq. There is nothing to go back to. There is more I could tell you but not now. I can't write about it any more here.

When I go to England, I will tell you the rest. We can sit in a café and then I will tell you all the rest there is to tell.

However, once people reached the UK, the difficulties of accessing higher education without loan access, as well as the intense uncertainties of waiting for status, could be problematic for even the most committed would-be students:

Eritrea (from Eritrea):
I like education very much, especially the invention and investigation of new things. In my childhood, when I started learning, I had a bright future in front of me to become a doctor or to become a professor. In England, I want to continue my education and I want to participate in higher levels of investigation. I dream of eradicating some of the challenges that people are facing. I would like to travel to every part of the UK to share my ideas with the people. Most of the southern people of the UK are facing the migration of people, and they have enough knowledge about that, but there are some people in the UK that do not have enough knowledge about this. I haven't had conversations with many people, but I have been told that education is better in southern UK. For education, Glasgow and Edinburgh are also better. For working, London and Birmingham are better. People say that. I really appreciate the people of UK; I am not speaking about the government, but the people. It wasn't my expectation that there would be a fence in Calais, put there by the UK government.

I educated myself. Learning means building on any part of your mind, it does not mean holding on to your culture. You have to eradicate the bad parts and keep the good parts. You have to be well talented. Learning does not mean counting grades and levels. It means you have to be well skilled. Your mind must think in a super manner. That is what learning means.

When I first got to the UK, I was in Liverpool for a while and I had a friend that I knew from before. He has lived in Liverpool for about six years. He is an Eritrean guy and he became my solicitor. He took me for the first screening interview. Now he is in Liverpool and I had an interview two months ago – and I am still waiting for my residence permit.

Refugees' Voice (from Afghanistan):
I would love to carry on with my studies and have my degree after maybe two or three years of struggling. Hopefully, I can be more of a professional person, as I would love to be. I am working now because I am eager to put myself on a good track, but study-wise I am a bit too lazy. Maybe once I get on track then I will be okay. I even registered online for one of the university classes of the online university for refugees, Kiron.[1] I did their test; but it is hard. Currently my life is hard and it is difficult to find the motivation – it has an effect on my discipline. But also not studying does affect me and if my asylum claim does work, I will be willing to go to the university; I will go in person this time not online.

---

1 Kiron is a worldwide online education network for refugees: https://kiron.ngo/.

In France, despite their uncertain asylum status, some authors were able to enrol in October 2016 in a degree foundation programme at the University of Lille. This programme has given the opportunity to 76 refugees who used to live in the 'Jungle' to become students for the 2016–17 academic year. Among them are Syrians, Afghans, Pakistanis and Sudanese. All the students were part of a special class to learn French. The aim is to provide them with enough language skills to carry on with their studies at the end of the year. Riaz expressed how he felt on beginning the course:

> *Riaz (from Pakistan):*
> It was my first day at the University of Lille today; it was a dream coming true for me. I am so happy. Tomorrow I have a meeting with the interior minister of France at the campus. I was selected to go by the university staff. Give me your suggestions to what I should discuss with him.

Giving help

Riaz used to be a refugee volunteer in the 'Jungle' for the organisation L'Auberge des Migrants, translating, and helping with access to medical and legal services. He also guided the work of many volunteers at the camp. He has continued similar work in Lille:

> *Riaz (from Pakistan):*
> Computers, laptops and mobile phones make everyone's life easy. If you do any paperwork or any official

work or studies, so you will do it in a shorter time than doing with your hands – for instance, preparing ideas, writing, reading or watching something. I have got some laptops from donations, and I hand them out to the students who were already selected for studying in Lille 3 University. They are so happy to study here in the university. This is their goal, to achieve things for themselves in the near future, and to make the future bright.

In order to help refugees in the UK, some authors have created, with others, a support organisation in the UK that aims to recreate the sense of community they used to have in Calais. The initiative, 'Hopetowns'[2] started in May 2016. The organisation aims to provide two-way support for both volunteers and refugees from the camp in Calais and anywhere in Europe:

Africa (from Sudan):
Myself and some friends are talking about making a support network: 'HopeTowns'. What I would like to do, when I get my status, is to use the talents that homeless people and refugees have, to help make a good environment for them. Refugees are not born refugees. Homeless people are not born homeless, or drug users; they need treatment and a place to live. There are many empty houses here that we could open up. We could also buy caravans. We need to distribute food to homeless people, not just to provide food banks. The people can provide support for each

2 https://www.facebook.com/hopetownsUK/

other because they know best what they need; all they require is somewhere to meet, and a little money for tea. We also want to have an Information Bus that can travel to all the towns in the UK, distributing information and discovering what the problems are and what is needed, so that people are not isolated and told 'just wait' when they come here. We could also receive calls from and give help to people arriving from, for instance, Calais. Already, we have some organisations that would work in partnership with us. We are making a database, and planning how to do this.

Refugees' Voice (from Afghanistan):
Hopetowns is about building refugee communities. When I was in Calais, I was already discussing it with my friends. I know that a grassroots network was relevant there but this is not happening here in the UK. Even though we see that there are plenty of other organisations like the Refugee Council or Refugees Welcome – they are doing similar kinds of things – but we think there is always a need. This is why we are trying to build refugee communities and to build a platform for refugees. Other platforms exist, but they are not refugee-led initiatives and basically what we are trying to do is something different. It is a refugee-led initiative which is already taking place at the grassroots level as was relevant in Calais. We are trying to provide mutual support for solidarity and friendship, and a platform where refugees can reunite. We can give some guidance and advise people as best as we can. It would not be only for refugees who went to Calais; the project we are doing is for every single refugee in

the UK to whom we could provide support and help. We are looking forward to being an organisation or an NGO that would be linked to many other organisations because we would love to work all together. In Calais, our aim was to work together and we know that there are hundreds of thousands of people who are working with refugees, or taking aid, or working as volunteers across the world. There are hundreds of organisations, but all these organisations are not one organisation. My dream would be to make only one organisation. I am still planning to make such an organisation. A bit like UNHCR, but led by refugees and run by both refugees and volunteers at the grassroots level, with the refugees working collaboratively and collectively. They can really bring something under one umbrella. Everyone could share their ideas. I see sometimes that one group is doing something on the one side and another group on the other side is doing the same thing. People from different organisations overstep each other, they cause each other problems. So I think it would be better if they can share their ideas; collectively, it would be much better.

The end of the Calais 'Jungle'

While many organisations acknowledged that the camp was not a decent place to live for refugees, they wished the authorities had organised the eviction in a better way. Some authors have been very vocal about the situation on the ground and have used social media to bear witness and to make their voices heard.

For instance, in mid-August 2016, an administrative court in Lille gave the decision that camp shops could not be closed by the police despite a call for months by the local prefecture to close them; following this decision, Babak, who is claiming asylum in France and who was at the time volunteering with a camp organisation, wrote:

> *Babak (from Iran):*
> The decision of the court is going well, the restaurants will still be alive, no demolition, no bulldozering! No stress. You can still find nan, Afghan espenaj, milk tea, Afghan omelette, you can go and celebrate today in cafes and restaurants.

A few days later, Babak reported the following:

> Police closed down the new tents that were built for the people at the École des Arts de Métiers (which had been burned down), and also they threw their stuff to the other side of the road. How rude and horrible!

As the announced end of the 'Jungle' drew near, Babak wrote about his friends, still trying:

> In the darkness of the night, with their covered and worried faces, they pass Calais streets.
> In small groups, everybody is going the same way, to the boat of dreams or maybe to the train of dreams.
> When the night and the silence absorbs Calais, my friends will just wake up. When the day will end for many people, they will start a new day.
> They will go to other side of the city. No one knows

how will the nights go by in Calais and how the morning will arise.

They will go fight with darkness, from darkness. How long will these wars continue? When will this city become a city?

Every day we will hear about the destruction of the 'Jungle', and my friends will be more hopeless. The space will become more narrow, more hopeless and more dangerous!

Many nights I hear the sound of the trucks and helicopters. Traffic, trucks, highway ! What a repetitive game. What a dangerous game.

You will hear these sounds all around Calais and you don't know how many lives will be at risk with each truck's horn.

World war will happen every night between my friends and the police. Yes, they are my friends because we understand each other, because we are victims of these wars and these politics.

We are those who know the pain of a worthless passport. We are those who carry the name of 'migrant' and 'refugee' for years. Those who feel the lashes of strange looks at our faces. They understand me, we come from behind the borders, all these barbed wire fences were made for us!

Calais is not a city for my friends. Here are their worst memories. These injustices will be with us for many years, like a stain that sticks on us.

These injustices come from before we were born. They started when these names first arose: Europe, Africa, America, Asia. 'So where were you born? Where do you come from?! No sorry, that way is closed for you. The police and the barbed wires are here just for you, go back!'

We should use the smuggling way! We should pass the hardest way. Like our tough backgrounds, like all the cruelties we fled from in our countries, here again and again and again. It's Always Hard work for pulled-hard people.

On the other hand, people are passing with their colourful passports, no barbed wires, no police. Calais is a beautiful coastal city for them. The only difference between them and us is that they were born in the right place. Perhaps they just pass by here and comment about the weather and the restaurants in Calais!

But Calais is a mysterious city. Calais is the most tired, and the biggest victim of these political games!

These are hard times for Calaisians too. It is like Calais's skin is formed by blood and bodies. Calais is also the victim of all these wars. All the endless wars between England and France many years ago, maybe now between my friends and the police. This war city still has war within.

Many people will come, many people leave, some will be disappointed, some have lost their families and some die and died, and their names will be lost between the ever continuous thread of news.

Stop all these wars, stop these games, Calais is tired, my friends are tired.

Babak is also part of this cohort of refugee students in Lille and what follows is a text he wrote after a few days at the university a few kilometres away from the camp that was at that time being dismantled:

I open my Facebook page and turn over it. I see myself burning in news. I'm becoming homeless, displaced; and with a bag on my back I'm going on an endless route!

And we, migrants for a lifetime, we leave again; but those fires in our houses are too familiar for us. How familiar are these pictures and footage?

Like bombs thrown in Syria or fire in Afghanistan's heart which everyone is feeding with barrels of gasoline. Indeed, this violence smells like our homelands. Like it's been written in our destinies. Yesterday our houses were bombed, today our shelters are on fire. When we left our countries, in our dreams we did not imagine our European days to be such painful days. That day when we packed our memories in a bag with a dream of freedom walking to Europe, how naive were we!

This journey taught me that our race is the race of pain and with this journey we just changed the kind of pain.

That day when I raised my voice for freedom, they answered with torture and prison. Here we shout, and no one hears. But the pain is the same. It is just hidden behind labels of freedom and equality.

That pain is like the chic man with a tie and a suit who raids our privacy and summarises us behind his fake headlines.

In my country, they had mullahs' dresses and their beards smelled of the blood of my liberal brothers. Here, they clean their mouths with pocket handkerchiefs.

In the midst of this, me and my brothers are like

marionettes in the hands of politics. Going up and down, and losing our springtime with these escapes. The pain is always with us, with different faces!

Watching videos of the Afghans dancing in the burning 'Jungle', I sob. Those Afghans who have war on their tables, and their skin wounded by those foreign governments. Those Afghans who have been migrants for years and have inherited war from their fathers. They are the epitome of resistance. Behind their proud faces and their dance, they hide their hardship. They gather all their pain from their homeland and wrap it up in a scarf with the colour of their flag around their necks. The pain strangles their necks, like the ropes strangle the young Iranians' necks when they get the answer to their shout for freedom from bullets, prison and hanging.

These days, the more I see and I think, the more my pain increases! But this time, these fires and failures burn my skin, part by part. The darkness of these fires will stay in my heart and its smudge will remain in my lungs. I know this will kill me one day! But what can I do except from making these papers black with writing, and screaming screams which nobody hears.

I didn't find my identity yet and I got lost walking around strangers: those who see my black hair and face and forget what I am inside.

I see some white people with dark minds, those whose forefathers were slave traffickers; and now they can't see a slave who became independent. Those who looted Africa and couldn't see Africans' warm hearts. These warm hearts have the same kind of pain as mine. These who have lion's skins and a heart as big as the Sahara. These who fight against racist pain and still make hope in my heart with their shiny smiles. Those who shared their meals with me and who, each time I walked by their tent, invited me for tea. These are the people who lost their families and friends in wars and in the Mediterranean Sea, but never lost their kindness and honour.

Yesterday they were sleeping under the hot sun of Africa and now they sleep in the cold streets of Europe, but their heart will always remain warm.

On social media, I am invited to watch film from refugee camps of women and children marching, those who shout for human rights in countries that call themselves 'humanitarian'. The children who should be in school now. Early this morning, they woke up with covered and frozen faces from the cold, and started protesting and demonstrating. Honestly, isn't this too early for them to start?

Sorry, kids, that you had to start that early going through political games. Please enjoy your childhood a bit. I know it's hard to hide your pain behind childish smiles. I don't want to disappoint you, but your voice won't be heard by the governments. They've been deaf for long time. They see us only in their TV frame.

Don't you remember that Syrian child who was taken out from bomb debris and put in an ambulance? Beaten in his face by the cameras flashes; after a few days, nobody heard about him again, but I still can hear the bombs falling in Syria!

Sorry kids, I wish I was there to hug you but I am also one who escaped from politics and now I too am looking for papers and a new identity.

My hands are tied and one after the other, they take us on stage. When I raise up my voice I am scared that maybe tomorrow Mr Judge will become fretful with my words and refuse my asylum case. Then again I would have to live some years without identity. I don't know what to do; but when I saw you, and my brothers' tents burning, I couldn't keep calm and 'like' such posts. I cried in my little room, and I built a world in my head that has a place for all of us. There is no need for your protests and my writings. Honestly, I don't know if my dream will come true or if their destructive hands will break my head like your hearts.

These days, I feel my pains are conflicting. I don't know whether I should have stayed in my country and endured the pain there, or whether I should indeed have come here to discover new pains and fight against them.

I don't know how long my pain will be able to write. Perhaps until the day when there will be no more homeless refugees, oppressed people, and children marching instead of going to school. As I'm writing, I'm burning. There is no escape; it's the last stop. Enough of being the servant for Gods of power.

Refugees' Voice wrote from another perspective about the eviction plan:

Refugees' Voice (from Afghanistan):
It is a tough time for everybody but to be honest, you have to think about it in both ways, 'Jungle' cannot be sustainable. The 'Jungle' used to exist and it will exist still, but the problem is that it was too much in the

media. The government did not like it to be too much in the media. That is why they wanted to remove the 'Jungle'; but somehow the 'Jungle' still continues, in some places, somewhere, as it used to exist for the last decade. Volunteers were always nice people, helping refugees, and this has always been appreciated. But in a way, if you think about it, people are not only looking for humanitarian support; people are looking for political support. Yet unfortunately, even if people are doing their very own best, despite this, they cannot make any political changes. However, if they remove the 'Jungle', this is for the government; but it will be good for the people as well.

Riaz actively raised awareness on social media about what was happening in the camp during its dismantling. He came back from Lille University to continue helping refugees:

Riaz (from Pakistan):
Monday 24 October. Hello everyone! Today is the first day of the dismantling. The police are surrounding Calais and the 'Jungle' from everywhere. We want the operation to go well, calmly and without any violence or problems. I hope that all of you guys will miss the 'Jungle'. This 'Jungle' will be a lot of good memories to all of us. Stay safe and keep in touch. We will always be here to talk.

Monday October 24 – evening. My heart was breaking today with every single one of my 'Jungle' friends and family who are still stuck in Calais. We all tried our best to get everyone out of the 'Jungle' but, sorry, we did not win the fight. I am so pleased for those who already left and made it on their own way: keep fighting. I am so blessed to have had you in my life. Every single one of you guys has suffered traumas that I cannot even comprehend. I cannot bear the thought of being away from my 'Jungle' friends and family, not knowing if they are safe. Wherever you end up, may you find peace, your own way, a normal and happy life, and sanctuary. Wherever you end up, they are lucky to have you. Wherever you end up, I still hope we get to meet again someday.

My eyes have been opened on this journey and I have learnt a lot from all of you guys. I realise how blessed we are and how much we take for granted. I wish people could see what I see. I am humbled by your life journey. I am in awe of your bravery; how many small and big troubles and problems haven't you faced? You guys are my heroes and forever true friends, throughout my entire life. Every single one of you.

Tuesday 25 October. Hello. Look at the police brutality around Calais city as well. The police are patrolling in Calais, and if they see refugees, they stop them and take them straight away to the detention centre.

It's a very terrible situation in the 'Jungle' now. Many of the refugees are waiting for the bus to go to the CAO centres. One of the Afghan men asked me if I could help to get him and his wife a ticket to go to Paris. I said, 'Yes of course I will help you guys, and it is for that that I am here, to help refugees in Calais.'

FIGURE 5.4
After the fires (after the first eviction, in March 2016).
Photo by Adam (from Sudan).

In the midst of the closure, Safia shared her anxiety of being sent to the countryside, far away from cities, which she believes provide more opportunities for her and her children to start a new life:

> *Safia (from Afghanistan):*
> We just want to go to the UK, because in the UK we can understand the language. It is an easy language and it is an international language. There are jobs. Another language is very difficult to learn, to understand the people and to understand what they are thinking. When you have to learn another language, it takes at least two to three years. We want to go to England because we understand English.
>
> We are also thinking about asylum in France;

maybe, once I will understand the language and the people, this will be better. French government officials came with a map, and showed me certain areas, but they were not cities. They showed it to us, and you had to decide, 'I could go there, there, and there in the countryside ... Toulon ... Toulon, yes, here.'

So they came to the camp and they said to us, 'It is this many hours to go here, and that many hours to go there.' We wanted Paris because it is a city, because they have hospitals. Cities have everything you need, and you can buy everything nearby, everything you need; but that is not true in the countryside. There is nothing.

I was a nurse and my husband a doctor. And I want to start my job again. My job is very respectable. It is a good job. We wanted to go the UK, but now it is hard and it is closed. Maybe we will be staying here; we don't know.

When the police come, we will stay here in the caravan, because we don't have another place to go; but if we have another place, then maybe we will go. We need a good life, we need good education and good health services. Here in Calais, it is not good, there is no school, there is no future.

I am not the only one to decide, I have to discuss it with my husband; but my neighbour went to a government accommodation centre and came back, saying it is not good. He said he got a very small room; the clothes washing facilities were also not good, and so he came back here. In fact, two or three families went to such housing, but they came back to the 'Jungle'.

Because of that, we don't really trust the system.

We want maybe to claim asylum but we don't know. People are talking, people come back here to the 'Jungle' and they want to stay here now.

I don't want to go to the countryside. In Afghanistan, I was living in a city. In a city, everything is possible. Especially for hospitals, where we could work. In the countryside, if you don't have a car, you can't do anything, you can't even go to the doctor. There are no jobs there. We want a life to enjoy, not a tiring life, Hopefully it will get better.

Reflecting on the 'Jungle' experience

Omer AKA Dream (from Sudan):

Call me dream, this is my name
Black moonlight in the dark night
Fabulous I cannot see the way
For moon rays reflecting
Of myriads of stars
In this I feel the colour purple
As rich as vineyards
With the flavours of rose
That sweep around my face
In a corridor of green grapes and seashells
So sad and melancholy
Full of lilting and deluding
Everything is satin yellow
Mirrored in my life's memory
Circles of joyous carnivals
Interrupted by friends left behind

Forever playing with the dolphins
Among the tempestuous seas
My sights are to return
To my heart made of ochre straw wood and clay
I see my lifetime's spirals
That appear as a night's dream
In midsummer, I awake
To find the veil of cloudy morns
Full of dew-soaked serrated green

The time spent in the 'Jungle' has been for many a place of learning about life, upon which some authors have decided to build on for their future. As Muhammad writes:

Muhammad (from Syria):
I think no man can enter the 'Jungle' and leave it in the same manner, without changing. There were so many friends. Some of them had been there for four to six months, others for three to four months. Everyone had their own stories and journeys which are greater than could be written in such pages as these. Each one has had his impact in your life. In the 'Jungle', I learned more about myself, by having new windows to look through.

Similarly, Ali wrote of making the best of a bad situation:

Ali (from Iran):
Good feelings of reconciliation: reconcile with your friend, reconcile with nature, with people, with yourself; reconcile with your life. The starting point of all these reconciliations and good feelings will come from

badness. Excessive goodness and sweetness can be disgusting, life needs bitterness sometimes.

I would like to be thankful for the badness around me in Calais, in Iran and the world. Because they directed me towards having the best viewpoint in my life yesterday. I saw a golden wheatfield and a sheaf of red flowers in the wind. That gold colour can be a symbol of money, power, the routine and the mechanical life, and those red flowers can be the symbol of love and freedom. If the golds did not exist, the red flowers wouldn't be beautiful that much!

So if badness did not exist, we could not find the pleasure of goodness and reconciliation with ourselves. I say thank you to badness that showed me beauty, it's you that always hides yourself under shadow of goodness. Today I tried the good feeling of reconciliation with badness.

Refugees' Voice remembered his time in Calais as a time where he was at peace with himself, and perhaps, where he learned what he needed to do in the UK:

Refugees' Voice (from Afghanistan):
I lived ten years in the UK, but maybe I haven't made such friendships as I did during six months in Calais. Many people volunteered in the 'Jungle' and many of them had good intentions; I know all the people that had good intentions. Maybe in the UK I would have searched for them and it would have taken me thirty years. I am still connected with every single one of them. My situation is tough as I told you, so I am trying to find my way, and this is why I am staying

away from everyone. I am really in a bad situation and I am trying to solve my own problems. One of the things I realised throughout all my journey is that I have always put people in front of me, and I never put myself first. I should have put myself first. Now if my situation was stable, I would be much stronger and I could have been in the situation where I could have helped much more people not only physically but even economically.

Some authors left Calais earlier than others; some went further away, and some are further along in the asylum process. Many are waiting for interviews, court cases, or decisions; some have started to receive answers. These 'new chapters' will mean other challenges of finding work, accommodation, and new networks, But Africa, like four other authors, has recently been granted Limited Leave to Remain in the UK:

Africa (from Sudan):
Finally, after a very long wait with much suffering but also new friendships that kept me going, I have today – thanking God – received my refugee status in UK. Thank you all brothers and sisters who stood by my side during this time. Now a new chapter can begin, inshallah.

CONCLUSION

Babak (from Iran):
Life is the very same moments that we waste to find happiness. All we need is to enjoy them. Happiness can be a comforting family. It can be a good friend. It can be a moment that we laugh. It does not have to be about money, a house, or a car. Happiness can be found in a wooden house, in the forest where two lovers live. Happiness can be the warmth of sunshine through the bedroom window. We have to remember that we can use all the moments of our life. We can build our life the way we want it. We have to break the borders inside us.

When I think about my journey and how I had to leave everything in my country, it was hard and I get sad. But when I return to my childhood, I remember that I dreamed about travelling around the world. Look where I am now! It is true that I have come here with much difficulty, but I travelled to a new world. I have experienced new cultures and seen new people. I learned a lot of good things. I am on my way towards my dreams!

All our dreams work in the same way. First we build them in our head. Then we build walls that are on the way to dreams. But if we don't think about these obstacles, we reach our dreams easily. In fact, there is nothing out of reach: we need to want it and work for it, to fight with the fears that stop us reaching it and beat them. It may take a bit of time but it will happen.

All it takes is wanting it to happen!

This book has brought together voices – stories and images – from a small fraction of the thousands of people stuck in the unofficial refugee camp near the crossing between Britain and France, the Calais 'Jungle', between autumn 2015 and autumn 2016.

For the authors, writing and taking photos for this book was largely an effort to reach a wider public, to tell them about all the different realities of the 'Jungle':

Haris (from Pakistan):
It is a very good idea to give cameras to different people in the camp. Each of them take hundreds of pictures in a day or in a week. For one person it is very hard to cover the whole 'Jungle'. But doing it in this way, 10,000 pictures are collected. One person can't do that alone.

Creating this programme is a very good idea so we can cover a lot about the 'Jungle'. Journalists come to show the world the condition in the 'Jungle' and to show that people need help: 'Please help these people, they are living in the "Jungle".' When someone hears the name 'Jungle', they think about animals, not human beings. Here in Calais there is a jungle, yes, but humans are living in the 'Jungle', so if you want to show that, you show the toilet conditions of the 'Jungle', the food conditions, the tents, clothes and shoes. You show them the people who are living in here. You show them the human life.

The book project was also, partly, in circumstances that were difficult and tedious, a way to continue studying, and to engage in a critical and creative process:

FIGURE C.I
Babak's self-portrait, 2016. Portrait by Babak (from Iran).

Babak (from Iran):
I think it is important with these kinds of projects because people need care and education. They can do photography to learn new things. Here you can sleep and eat everyday but not really care what you do, but it is really good to learn new things, for example in a school, like a photography class, or a movie class.

For many authors, writing for this book has been an opportunity to reflect on the lives they have had, the journeys that brought them here, the circumstances the authors found themselves in and the futures they are imagining. Despite the difficulties remembering and writing down the stories they wished to tell, too, for both Shaheen and Mani, the thought of someone reading these stories made the experience worthwhile:

FIGURE C.2

So then I took a photo. It was a rainy day. I was sitting inside my restaurant. It is a little bit blurry and that is because of the plastic covering the window. Outside is the rain and I was sitting inside, which is also why it is a little bit blurry. Photo by Haris (from Pakistan).

Shaheen (from Afghanistan):

When writing, I found it hard to remember some things. It was helpful to have someone editing my English. And it was interesting to write, especially because I knew that now, many people would read my story.

Mani (from Iran):

Producing the work for this book was like looking at the car mirror when you are driving; looking to a part of your life in the past with all the good and the bad. Maybe we have more time to think about our situation now; our experiences, our feelings, our actions.

It was difficult, because we had to write in a language

which we didn't have enough knowledge about. It was easy, because we had to write in a language we hadn't enough knowledge about so that nobody expected us to write a brilliant text.

It was difficult, because we had to remember a part of our life in the past. It was easy, because we had to remember a part of our life in the past.

It was hard, because we have a lot of painful memories there in the past. It was easy, because we have a lot of wonderful memories there.

I think it was hard but beautiful, like flying up to the sky and looking down to the part of your life on the land.

There was too much to remember, because we lived there, in the writing, all of our life; moments, seconds. There wasn't anything to remember, because we learned in the 'Jungle' life to forget everything, to leave all our memories.

Maybe a child, a girl, a stranger will read this book on a faraway mountain in Scotland. Maybe my brother will read this book, in my home.

In the book, the authors have reflected on their lives before arriving in the 'Jungle', on their long journeys that brought them here, life in the 'Jungle' and the futures they imagine and hope for. The book is not just a book about the authors. *Voices from the 'Jungle'* is about humanity, global injustice and the roles we all play in creating them.

Africa suggests that we end this book with a quote from Charlie Chaplin's speech in his 1940 film *The Great Dictator*:[1]

---

1 *The Great Dictator,* 1940, dir. Charlie Chaplin.

I'm sorry, but I don't want to be an emperor. That's not my business. I don't want to rule or conquer anyone. I should like to help everyone – if possible – Jew, Gentile – black man – white. We all want to help one another. Human beings are like that. We want to live by each other's happiness – not by each other's misery. We don't want to hate and despise one another. In this world, there is room for everyone. And the good earth is rich and can provide for everyone. The way of life can be free and beautiful, but we have lost the way.

The authors' words resonate with the same messages of freedom, democracy and solidarity, and the last word shall be with them:

Eritrea (from Eritrea):
In my conclusion, first of all I would like to thank my lord Jesus Christ who is always beside me and then my family, especially my father and my mother who led me to be a perfect person. Finally, I would like to appreciate those who helped me to pass the difficulties and those who are still helping me, my lovely friends. I wish peace to the whole world and for those who are in desperate paths to settle. Wishes of Solidarity among people of the world. God is good.

Ali (from Iran):
At night in the 'Jungle', fights would start between the police and the people.

Beyond the bridge, the rules change and the power is in the hands of the strong ones.

It is like a Hollywood movie sometimes, movies like

FIGURE C.3
The bridge. Photo by Ali (from Iran).

B13 [*Banlieue 13*], where bad people control parts of a city and the police try to deal with them. Maybe the hero of this movie is a good policeman who comes and wipes clean all the filth and vice from the city.

But this is not a Hollywood movie or a tale with a hero. This is the 'Jungle' with thousands of people of a hundred different nationalities, opinions and faiths.

No movie, no picture, no book can show the extent of the tragedy. You need to see it and live it!

The hero of this tale isn't a policeman. Here, everybody is their own hero, for fighting, trying to survive and follow their dreams.

The people of this city fall in love, learn, live and try to help.

Maybe some of them cheat, thieve, break the law and damage the city, but these bad things are not coming from their nature. These people are victims of the third world, and the third world exists because there is a first world!